RevMarketing Playbook
For Hotels

Unlocking revenue potential through innovative marketing and revenue strategies.

Copyright © 2024 by Userguest B.V.

All rights reserved.

No portion of this book may be reproduced in any form without written permission from the publisher or author, except as permitted by copyright law.

Contents

About This Book v

The RevMarketing Concept vi

The Hotel Website 1
    The Digital Landscape of the Hospitality Industry 2
    Building a High-Converting Hotel Website 6
    Website Design Best Practices for Hotels 6
    Optimising Website Navigation and User Flow 9
    Creating Engaging and Persuasive Content 11
    Website Analytics & RevMarketing 13
    Introduction to Website Analytics 14
    Key Metrics for Hotel Website Analytics 17
    Exploring the Key KPIs–Website Traffic, Click
    Rate & Conversion Rate 20
    Your Website Analytics Check List 24
    The Relationship between Website Analytics and
    Revenue Management Strategies: 26
    Chapter 1: Key Takeaways 28

Understanding Your Guests' Booking Behaviour 30
    Why is Booking Behaviour Imrportant? 31
    Key Booking Behaviour Analysis 33
    Identifying Touchpoints and Optimising User Experience ... 36
    Personalisation through Booking Behaviour Analysis 37
    Personalising the Experience: Practical Tips 39
    Chapter 2: Key Takeaways 42

Revenue Management Fundamentals 44

    Understanding Revenue Management Principles
    and Pricing Strategies 45

    Pricing Strategies in Revenue Management 46

    The Revenue Management Cycle 49

    Market Segmentation and Demand Analysis 51

    Dynamic Pricing and Revenue Management Systems 54

    Chapter 3: Key Takeaways 55

    Conclusion 56

Practical Strategies to Drive Incremental Revenue Through the Hotel Website 57

    Practical Strategies 58

Technology and Automation in the Hotel Industry 62

    The Power of Technology and Automation 63

    Macro-Data and Micro-Data: Unveiling Insights
    for Revenue and Marketing 66

    Integration for Revenue and Marketing Enhancement 68

    Conclusion 69

    The Interplay of Tools: Orchestrating Data for
    Optimal Results 69

    RevMarketing Automation 72

    Chapter 5: Key Takeaways 77

Mastering RevMarketing for Hotel Revenue Excellence 79

About This Book

In today's fiercely competitive hospitality industry, the difference between thriving and merely surviving lies in mastering revenue management and executing targeted marketing strategies. This book has been meticulously crafted for hoteliers looking to navigate these challenging waters with confidence and precision.

"*Unlocking Hotel Revenue Potential: A RevMarketing Playbook* is your comprehensive guide to unlocking the potential of RevMarketing and harnessing it as a powerful tool to optimise your hotel's profitability.

Throughout these pages, you will embark on a journey that demystifies the RevMarketing concept, providing you with a deep understanding of its principles. More importantly, you will learn how to craft and execute revenue-driven marketing strategies that are finely tuned to suit the unique requirements of your hotel.

By the final chapter, you'll be armed with the skills and insights needed to seamlessly integrate RevMarketing into your hotel operations. Not only will you transform your approach to revenue generation, but you will also gain a newfound proficiency and readiness to conquer the competitive landscape of the hospitality industry.

The RevMarketing Concept

RevenueMarketing, or RevMarketing, is a strategic approach that combines marketing and revenue management techniques to optimise a hotel's financial performance. It focuses on driving revenue growth and maximising profitability by aligning marketing efforts with revenue objectives.

RevMarketing involves leveraging data-driven insights and market intelligence to develop targeted marketing campaigns and pricing strategies. It goes beyond traditional marketing tactics by integrating revenue management principles and tactics into the marketing process.

RevMarketing is the art of seamlessly intertwining marketing efforts with revenue objectives, ushering in a new era of revenue growth and profitability. Gone are the days of siloed strategies; instead, RevMarketing harmonises data-driven insights and market intelligence, channelling them into precision-crafted marketing campaigns and pricing strategies. This is where the alchemy of RevMarketing occurs, unleashing a potent synergy that takes your hotel to new heights.

Prepare to transcend the conventional as we delve into the world of RevenueMarketing. This groundbreaking approach transcends traditional marketing tactics by integrating the very principles and tactics of revenue management into the very fabric of the marketing process. The result? A hotel that not only attracts guests but also optimises revenue streams with unprecedented finesse.

Welcome to the future of hotel profitability—welcome to the RevMarketing Revolution.

1

The Hotel Website

In the rapidly evolving landscape of the hospitality industry, the hotel website has emerged as a pivotal direct booking channel, proving to be of paramount importance for hoteliers worldwide. As travellers increasingly turn to the internet to plan and book their accommodation, a well-designed and user-friendly hotel website serves as a virtual gateway to the property, offering a host of benefits to both guests and hotel owners.

The hotel website provides an opportunity for hotels to establish a strong online presence and showcase their unique offerings.

First and foremost, a **hotel website provides an opportunity for hotels to establish a strong online presence and showcase their unique offerings.** Through engaging content, high-quality images and immersive virtual tours, hotels can create an enticing digital experience that captivates potential guests and sets them apart from their competitors. The website serves as a digital brochure, allowing hoteliers to highlight their amenities, services, local attractions and room types. All of these factors play a crucial role in influencing a traveller's decision-making process.

Moreover, **direct bookings through the hotel website empower hoteliers with greater control over their revenue streams and guest relationships.** By bypassing third-party online travel agencies (OTAs), hotels can avoid hefty commission fees, thus maximising their profitability. Additionally, direct bookings grant hotels direct access to customer data, enabling them to personalise marketing efforts, offer tailored promotions and establish long-term guest loyalty.

Furthermore, a hotel website facilitates **seamless communication between the hotel and guests**. By incorporating live chat features or contact forms, hotels can provide prompt responses to inquiries, address concerns and offer personalised assistance throughout the booking process. This interactive and responsive approach helps build a positive guest experience even before their arrival, encouraging brand loyalty and positive word-of-mouth referrals.

The Digital Landscape of the Hospitality Industry

Within this section, we embark on a journey through the ever-evolving digital realm of the hospitality industry. Our mission is to decipher the intricate tapestry of trends and challenges that have left an indelible mark on how modern travellers go about booking their accommodations.

As we embark on this exploration, we will peel back the layers of the digital landscape to uncover the nuances of online booking behaviour.

By immersing ourselves in the current situation, we gain a profound understanding of the forces driving the decisions of today's travellers.

But our journey doesn't stop there. In this section, we shine a spotlight on a pivotal player in this digital orchestra: the hotel website. We'll unveil the crucial role it plays as a direct booking channel, illuminating the path for hotels to optimise their online presence and capitalise on the digital revolution sweeping the hospitality industry.

Understanding the Hospitality Industry Shift

In recent years, the hospitality industry has experienced a significant shift due to the widespread adoption of digital technology. With the rise of the internet and mobile devices, travellers now have unprecedented access to information, making them increasingly reliant on digital platforms for planning and booking their trips.

Online travel agencies (OTAs) have capitalised on this trend, offering travellers a one-stop-shop for comparing hotel options and making reservations. As a result, hotels have faced challenges in maintaining control over their booking channels and customer relationships.

The Power of Direct Bookings

USER ◉ GUEST

Direct bookings refer to reservations made directly through a hotel's official website or reservation system, bypassing third-party intermediaries like OTAs. These direct bookings hold immense significance for hoteliers.

Firstly, they allow hotels to retain control over their pricing, inventory and brand image, reducing dependency on third-party channels and avoiding hefty commission fees.

Secondly, direct bookings provide hotels with valuable customer data, enabling them to personalise offerings and marketing efforts, fostering long-term guest loyalty.

The Role of the Hotel Website

The hotel website serves as a virtual storefront, representing the property's identity and offerings in the digital world.

A well-designed and user-friendly website is essential for attracting and engaging potential guests.

Through compelling visuals, intuitive navigation and informative content, hotel websites can create immersive experiences that showcase the property's unique features, amenities and local attractions. The website acts as the primary touchpoint for guests during their research and booking process, making a lasting impression that influences their decisions.

Engaging Guests in the Digital Age

In the digital age, guests expect a seamless and personalised booking experience. Understanding guest behaviour and preferences is crucial for crafting a website that caters to their needs.

User experience (UX) is paramount with mobile responsiveness, fast loading times and easy-to-use interfaces becoming prerequisites for guest engagement. By embracing innovative technologies like smart pop-ups, virtual tours and chatbots, hotels can provide interactive and informative experiences, ensuring that guests feel confident in their decision to book directly.

Navigating Challenges and Competition

While direct bookings offer numerous benefits, hotels must navigate challenges in a competitive online landscape. OTAs continue to dominate search engine results, making it vital for hotels to optimise their online visibility and search engine rankings. Building brand awareness and loyalty requires strategic marketing efforts that drive traffic to the hotel website. By analysing successful case studies and industry trends, hoteliers can identify opportunities to stand out from the competition and capture more direct bookings.

Embracing a Direct Booking Mindset

For hotels to thrive in the digital era, it is crucial to instil a direct booking mindset within the organisation. This involves aligning the entire team with the goal of driving direct bookings and understanding the benefits that come with them. Setting measurable goals and key performance indicators (KPIs) allows hotels to track their progress and make data-driven decisions to optimise direct booking strategies continuously.

Armed with a comprehensive understanding of the digital landscape and the role of hotel websites in driving direct bookings, you are now ready to explore the essential elements of building an irresistible hotel website.

Building a High-Converting Hotel Website

In this section, our focus narrows, honing in on the artistry of building a hotel website that doesn't just stand out but excels in the realm of conversion.

Our mission here is clear: to equip you with the tools and knowledge needed to create a high-converting hotel website that not only captures the wandering eyes of potential guests but also convinces them to make direct bookings with your establishment.

To achieve this, we will delve deep into the world of website design, uncovering best practices that elevate your site's visual appeal and functionality. But that's just the beginning. We will also explore optimisation techniques that ensure your website operates at peak performance, offering visitors a seamless experience.

And it's not just about the aesthetics and mechanics. We recognise that content is king in the digital realm, and we will guide you through the art of crafting persuasive and engaging content that resonates with your target audience.

By the end of this section, you'll have the expertise to weave all these elements together, creating an online presence that doesn't just inform but captivates, persuades and ultimately drives direct bookings for your hotel.

Website Design Best Practices for Hotels

In this section, we will explore website design best practices specifically tailored to hotels.

A visually appealing and user-friendly website not only attracts potential guests but also enhances their overall experience, encouraging them to explore your property further and ultimately make a direct booking.

Website Design Best Practices

- USER / GUEST
- Booking Process Simplicity
- Room And Amenities Information
- Brand Identity
- Guest Reviews And Testimonials
- Captivating Homepage
- Clear CTAs
- User-Friendly Navigation
- Mobile Responsiveness
- Website Speed
- Visual Content

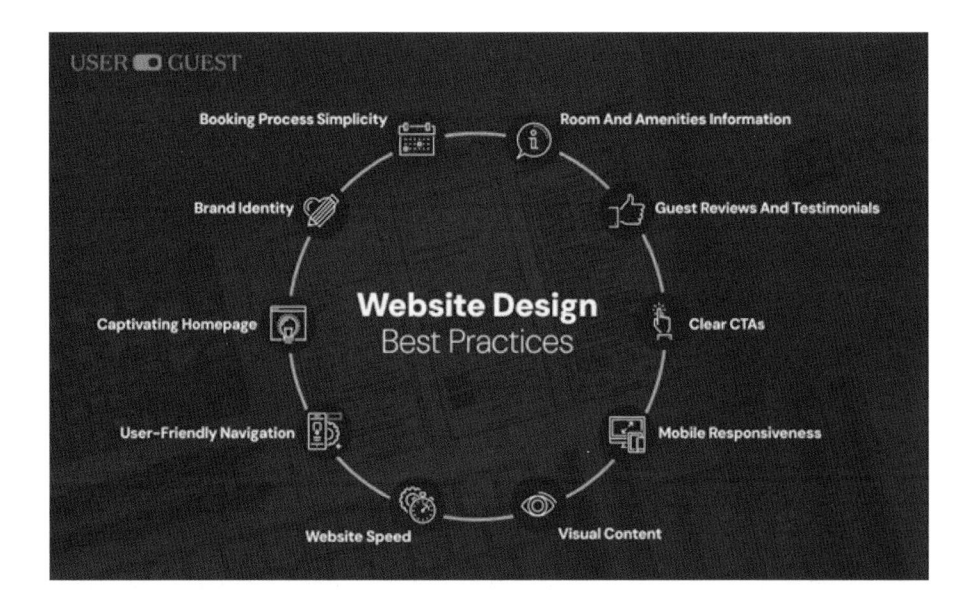

> **Understand Your Brand Identity**: Before delving into the design process, it's essential to have a clear understanding of your hotel's brand identity. Your website should reflect the essence of your brand, including its personality, values and unique selling points. Use consistent branding elements such as logos, colour schemes and fonts across your website to reinforce brand recognition and trust.

> **Create a Captivating Homepage:** Your homepage is the virtual entrance to your hotel, and it must make a strong impression. Use high-quality images and visuals that showcase the best aspects of your property. Consider using sliders or image carousels to highlight key amenities, services or promotions. Engage visitors with a captivating headline that conveys your hotel's unique value proposition.

> **Prioritise User-Friendly Navigation**: Ensure that your website's navigation is intuitive and user-friendly. Organise your menu items logically, making it easy for visitors to find the information they seek. Consider using dropdown menus to categorise information effectively. Include a prominent and easily accessible booking button on each page to streamline the booking process.

- **Optimise Website Speed**: Website speed is critical for user experience and search engine rankings. Compress images and utilise caching to reduce page loading times. Visitors are less likely to stay on a site that takes too long to load, which can lead to lost bookings. Regularly monitor your website's speed and make improvements as needed.

- **Emphasise Visual Content**: High-quality images and videos play a crucial role in engaging potential guests. Showcase your hotel's rooms, amenities, dining options and local attractions through visually appealing content. Use professional photographs and videos to create an immersive experience for visitors.

- **Mobile Responsiveness**: With an increasing number of users browsing on mobile devices, it is vital to ensure that your website is fully responsive across various screen sizes. Test your website on different devices to ensure that all elements are displayed correctly and that the user experience remains seamless.

- **Utilise Clear Calls-to-Action (CTAs)**: Guide visitors toward desired actions, such as booking a room or signing up for a newsletter, with clear and strategically placed CTAs. Use action-oriented language that encourages immediate engagement. Consider using contrasting colours to make CTAs stand out from the rest of the page.

- **Highlight Guest Reviews and Testimonials**: Build trust with potential guests by prominently displaying positive guest reviews and testimonials. Social proof can significantly influence a visitor's decision to book with your hotel. Showcase guest feedback and ratings on your homepage and throughout your website.

- **Provide Detailed Room and Amenities Information**: Offer comprehensive and detailed information about your hotel's rooms, suites and amenities. Use descriptive text and images to help guests envision their stay at your property. Highlight unique amenities and features that set your hotel apart from competitors.

> **Ensure Booking Process Simplicity**: Streamline the booking process to reduce friction and encourage conversions. A simple, user-friendly booking form with clear instructions and secure payment options will increase the likelihood of completing a direct booking.

Optimising Website Navigation and User Flow

One of the most critical aspects of creating a high-converting hotel website is optimising its navigation and user flow.

A well-structured website that allows visitors to find information effortlessly and move seamlessly through the booking process significantly improves the user experience and increases the likelihood of direct bookings. In this section, we will delve deeper into the key strategies for optimising website navigation and user flow.

> **Streamline Menu Structure**: Start by organising your website's menu items clearly and logically. Keep the menu structure simple and avoid overwhelming visitors with too many options. Utilise dropdown menus to categorise information into relevant sections, such as "Rooms & Suites", "Amenities", "Dining", "Events" and "Contact". This helps visitors quickly find what they are looking for without having to navigate through numerous pages.

> **Prominently Display Booking CTA**: Place a prominent and visually appealing "Book Now" or "Check Availability" call-to-action (CTA) button in strategic locations throughout your website. Ideally, this CTA should be easily accessible from any page, so visitors can initiate the booking process at any point during their browsing.

> **Implement Clear and Descriptive Labels**: Ensure that all navigation labels and menu items are clear, concise and descriptive. Avoid using ambiguous terms that might confuse visitors. For example, instead of using a vague label like "Services", be specific and use "Spa & Wellness" or "Meeting & Event Spaces".

- **Optimise the Booking Path**: The booking process should be as streamlined and straightforward as possible. Eliminate unnecessary steps and form fields that might deter users from completing their bookings. A single-page booking form with only essential information required is more likely to lead to higher conversion rates.

- **Provide Quick Access to Contact Information**: Make it easy for visitors to find your hotel's contact information. Display your phone number and email address prominently, preferably in the header or footer of every page. Quick access to contact details helps potential guests reach out for inquiries or assistance, which can boost their confidence in booking with your hotel.

- **Optimise for Mobile Navigation**: Given the increasing number of users accessing websites on mobile devices, it is crucial to ensure that your website's navigation is mobile-friendly. Test your site on various devices to ensure that menus and CTAs are easily accessible and user-friendly on smartphones and tablets.

- **Utilise Internal Links**: Internal linking refers to linking relevant pages within your website. By strategically placing internal links, you can guide visitors to related content, encouraging them to explore more areas of your site. This not only improves navigation but also helps with SEO by enhancing website structure and promoting deeper engagement.

- **Conduct User Testing**: Perform user testing with real individuals to identify any pain points or usability issues with your website's navigation and user flow. Collect feedback and make iterative improvements based on the users' experiences and suggestions.

Creating Engaging and Persuasive Content

Creating engaging and persuasive content is a crucial aspect of building a high-converting hotel website. Compelling content not only captures the attention of potential guests but also influences their decision-making process, encouraging them to choose your hotel over competitors.

In this section, we will explore various content strategies to effectively engage your audience and drive direct bookings.

- **Know Your Audience:** Before crafting content, it's essential to understand your target audience and their preferences. Conduct market research to identify the needs, desires, and pain points of your potential guests. Tailor your content to address their specific interests, such as highlighting family-friendly amenities for families or emphasising business facilities for corporate travellers.

- **Craft Persuasive Copywriting:** Use persuasive and enticing language to communicate the unique benefits and experiences that your hotel offers. Showcase your property's strengths, such as breathtaking views, luxurious amenities, or proximity to popular attractions. Focus on the value your hotel brings to guests, addressing the "what's in it for me" question that often arises in a potential guest's mind.

- **Create Captivating Headlines:** Headlines are the first point of contact with your audience. Craft attention-grabbing headlines that pique curiosity and compel visitors to read further. Use powerful words and phrases that evoke emotions and create a sense of urgency, such as "Unforgettable Getaway: Book Now and Save!" or "Limited-Time Offer: Exclusive Spa Package".

- **Utilise Visuals Effectively**: Accompany your written content with high-quality visuals that showcase your hotel's unique features. Use professional photographs and videos to convey the ambience, beauty, and experience that guests can expect during their stay. Visual content has a profound impact on emotional engagement and can significantly influence booking decisions.

- **Highlight Unique Selling Points (USPs)**: Identify your hotel's Unique Selling Points (USPs) and make sure they are prominently featured in your content. Whether it's your award-winning restaurant, state-of-the-art spa or stunning rooftop pool, these unique features help differentiate your property from competitors and entice potential guests to choose your hotel.

- **Provide Local Area Information**: Many guests are interested in exploring the local area during their stay. Provide information about nearby attractions, popular restaurants and events to enhance their travel experience. By offering local area guides and recommendations, you demonstrate your hotel's dedication to ensuring guests have a memorable stay.

- **Incorporate Social Proof**: Leverage social proof to build trust and credibility. Display guest reviews and testimonials on your website, showcasing positive experiences from past guests. Encourage satisfied guests to share their experiences on social media or review platforms, further enhancing your hotel's reputation.

- **Create a Sense of Urgency**: Encourage immediate action by creating a sense of urgency in your content. Utilise phrases such as "Limited Availability", "Book Now and Save", or "Exclusive Offer for a Limited Time Only". A sense of urgency can prompt potential guests to make a reservation sooner rather than later.

- **Offer Personalisation**: Use data from previous guest stays to personalise content for returning visitors. Offer special promotions or loyalty rewards based on their preferences and past interactions with your hotel. Personalised content makes guests feel valued and fosters a sense of loyalty.

Armed with a wealth of knowledge and an array of strategies, you are now fully equipped to embark on the journey of building a hotel website that not only captures the hearts of potential guests but also guides them towards the path of direct bookings.

Throughout this section, we've delved into the intricacies of website design where we've uncovered the secrets of best practices that will elevate your website's visual appeal and functionality. You've also honed your skills in optimising navigation and user flow, ensuring that visitors to your site experience nothing short of seamless satisfaction.

Moreover, we've demystified the art of creating content that not only informs but engages and persuades. Your ability to craft compelling narratives and messages will be the cornerstone of your website's ability to resonate with your target audience.

As you move forward, always bear in mind that your website is more than just a digital presence; it's a powerful tool. It holds the potential to unlock increased revenue streams and enhance guest satisfaction, two essential elements in the success of your hotel. So, with this newfound knowledge and confidence, step boldly into the world of online hospitality where every click can translate into a satisfied guest and a flourishing bottom line.

Website Analytics & RevMarketing

Within the world of RevMarketing, the key to unlocking its potential lies in the treasure trove of data offered by website analytics.

This section delves into the invaluable insights that emerge from customer data and booking patterns, insights that hold the key to identifying lucrative revenue opportunities, understanding customer segments and deciphering demand patterns.

As we navigate the digital landscape, we recognise that user behaviour on your website is akin to a roadmap to success. Every click, every browse and every preferred offer paints a vivid picture of your audience's desires and intentions. In the realm of RevMarketing, we harness this data to identify the pivotal touchpoints where revenue and marketing beautifully intersect.

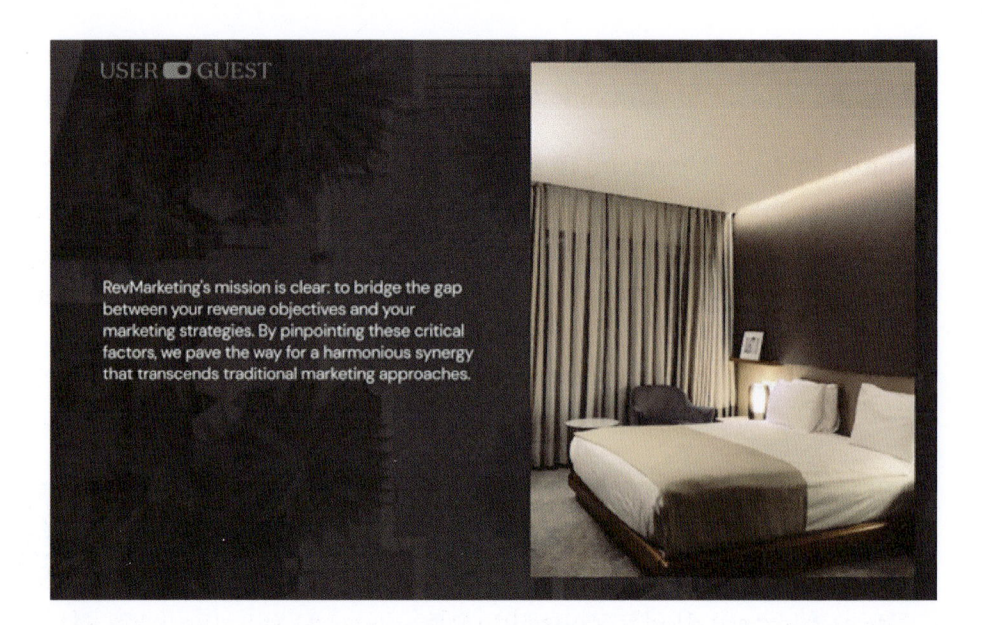

Now, it's time to roll up our sleeves and dive deep into the metrics that wield the most significant impact on direct bookings. These are the metrics that will guide your RevMarketing journey, ensuring that every action you take is purposeful and results-driven.

Introduction to Website Analytics

Website analytics refers to the process of collecting, measuring, analysing and interpreting data related to the performance of a website. It involves tracking various user interactions and behaviours on the website to gain valuable insights into how visitors engage with the content and features. Website analytics play a crucial role in helping hotel websites understand their audience, evaluate the effectiveness of marketing efforts, optimise user experience and drive direct bookings.

Why is it crucial for hotel websites?

- **Understanding User Behaviour**: Website analytics provides valuable data about how users navigate through the hotel website, what pages they visit, how long they stay on each page and where they drop off. This data helps hotels identify user preferences, pain points and areas of interest, enabling them to tailor the website to better meet guest needs.

- **Optimising User Experience**: By analysing website analytics, hotels can uncover usability issues and optimise the website's design and layout for a seamless user experience. User-friendly websites lead to higher engagement, longer sessions and increased chances of direct bookings.
- **Tracking Marketing Efforts**: Website analytics allow hotels to track the performance of their marketing campaigns. By understanding which marketing channels drive the most traffic and conversions, hotels can allocate their marketing budget more effectively and focus on strategies that yield the best results.
- **Measuring Conversion Rate**: A conversion rate is a critical metric that indicates the percentage of website visitors who complete a desired action, such as making a reservation or signing up for a newsletter. Website analytics help hotels measure their conversion rate and identify areas for improvement in the booking process.
- **Assessing Website Performance**: Website analytics tools provide data on website load times, page errors, and overall website performance. This information is vital for identifying technical issues that may hinder user experience and ensuring that the website operates smoothly.
- **Competitive Analysis**: Website analytics allow hotels to compare their website performance against competitors in the industry. By benchmarking against other hotels, they can identify strengths, weaknesses and opportunities for improvement.

Website analytics tools:

- **Google Analytics**: Google Analytics is one of the most widely used website analytics tools. It offers a comprehensive suite of features that enable hotels to track website traffic, user behaviour, conversions and more. Hotels can set up custom reports, track goals and implement event tracking to gain in-depth insights into user interactions.

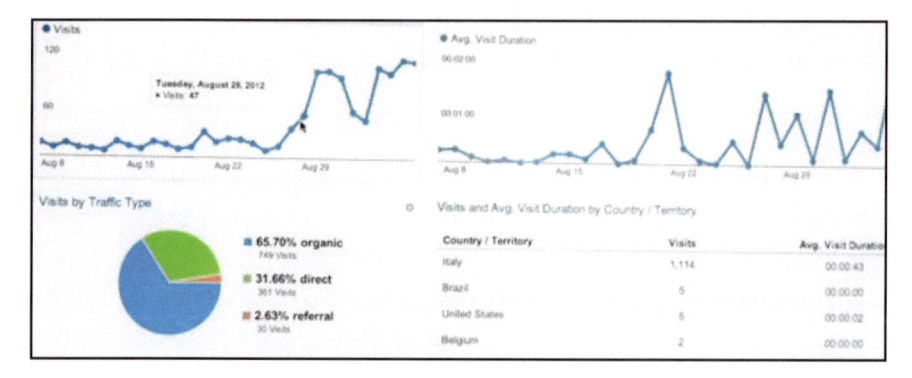

- **Hotjar:** Hotjar is a powerful tool that provides visual analytics, including heatmaps, session recordings and user feedback. Heatmaps display areas of the website that receive the most clicks, taps and scrolling, helping hotels understand user engagement.

- **Adobe Analytics:** Adobe Analytics is an enterprise-level analytics platform that offers advanced data tracking and segmentation capabilities. It allows hotels to create customised reports, measure the impact of marketing campaigns and gain a deeper understanding of customer behaviour.

- **Mixpanel:** Mixpanel is a user-centric analytics tool that focuses on tracking individual user actions and behaviour. Hotels can use Mixpanel to understand user journeys, engagement patterns and retention rates.

- **Crazy Egg:** Crazy Egg specialises in heatmaps and A/B testing. Hotels can use this tool to visually analyse user interactions and conduct A/B tests to compare different website variations for optimal performance.

In closing, we've unravelled the significance of website analytics in the realm of successful hotel websites. It's become abundantly clear that data-driven insights, extracted through the lenses of powerful analytics tools, hold the key to unlocking a world of opportunities.

For hotels, the advantages are manifold. Website analytics empowers them to fine-tune the user experience, offering a pathway to perfection. It enables them to not only track the efficacy of their marketing endeavours but also to quantify success through the lens of conversion rates. In this data-rich environment, hotels are poised to make informed decisions, guiding them toward the ultimate goal: driving direct bookings.

In this dynamic landscape, understanding user behaviour and preferences isn't a luxury; it's a necessity. It's a continuous journey of improvement, a perpetual quest to enhance guest satisfaction and a relentless pursuit of a competitive edge in the fiercely competitive hospitality industry.

In the end, it's not just about numbers and statistics. It's about the art of turning data into delight, transforming clicks into bookings, and crafting an online experience that leaves guests not just satisfied but longing to return. And in this journey, website analytics is the guiding light, illuminating the path to digital excellence for hotels around the world.

Key Metrics for Hotel Website Analytics

In the digital age, data reigns supreme, and for hotels seeking to excel in their online presence, website analytics is the compass guiding their voyage. Within this section, we embark on a journey through the intricate web of metrics known as key performance indicators (KPIs) that illuminate the performance of hotel websites and online marketing endeavours.

These KPIs are the storytellers of the digital realm, narrating tales of attraction, engagement, conversion and revenue generation. They form the backbone of strategic decision-making, helping hotels gauge the effectiveness of their digital strategies and paving the way for continuous improvement.

So, fasten your seatbelts as we dive deep into the world of hotel website analytics, unravelling the significance of each KPI. Together, we'll uncover how these metrics transform data into actionable insights, steering hotels toward the digital excellence that propels them ahead in the competitive landscape of the hospitality industry.

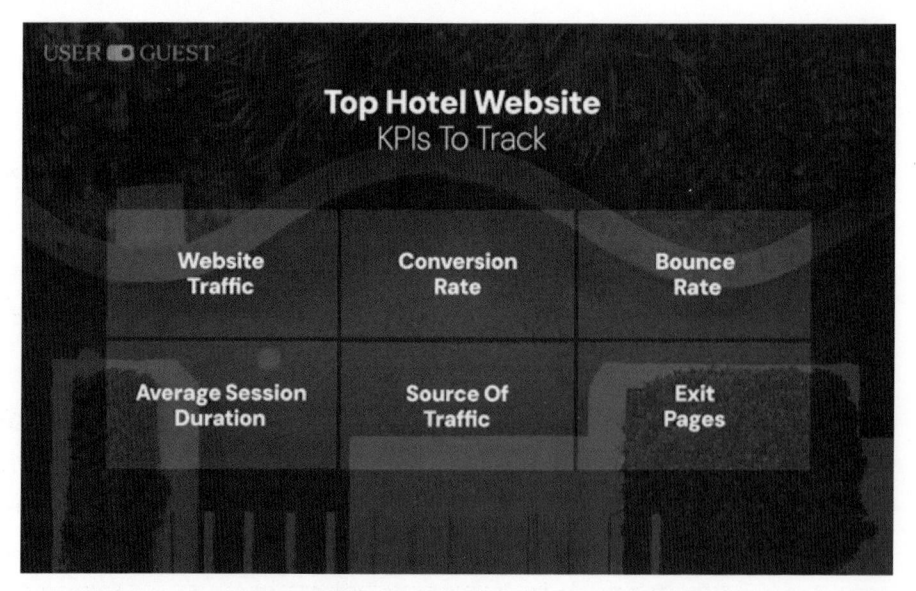

Top Hotel Website KPIs To Track

Website Traffic	Conversion Rate	Bounce Rate
Average Session Duration	Source Of Traffic	Exit Pages

- **Website Traffic**: Website traffic is a fundamental metric that measures the total number of visitors who access the hotel website over a specific period. It is essential for understanding the website's reach and popularity. Tracking website traffic allows hotels to identify trends in visitor volume, evaluate the impact of marketing campaigns and measure the website's overall visibility.

- **Conversion Rate**: The conversion rate represents the percentage of website visitors who complete a desired action, such as making a direct booking, submitting a contact form or signing up for a newsletter. For hotels, the primary conversion goal is often direct bookings. A high conversion rate indicates that the website effectively encourages visitors to take the desired action, resulting in more direct bookings and increased revenue.

- **Bounce Rate**: The bounce rate refers to the percentage of website visitors who leave the site after viewing only one page, without engaging further or navigating to other pages. A high bounce rate may indicate that visitors are not finding what they were looking for or that the website's content and design need improvement. Reducing the bounce rate is crucial for keeping visitors engaged and increasing the chances of conversion.

- **Average Session Duration**: Average session duration measures the average time visitors spend on the hotel website during a single session. A longer average session duration indicates higher user engagement and interest in the website's content. By analysing the average session duration, hotels can identify which pages or sections of the website attract the most engagement and focus on enhancing content in other areas.

- **Source of Traffic:** Understanding the source of website traffic is essential for evaluating the effectiveness of marketing channels and campaigns. Common traffic sources include organic search (visitors who find the website through search engines), direct traffic (visitors who type the website URL directly), referral traffic (visitors who come from external websites) and paid traffic (visitors from paid advertising campaigns). By tracking traffic sources, hotels can allocate marketing resources strategically and optimise their marketing efforts.

- **Exit Pages**: Exit pages indicate the last page visitors view before leaving the website. Analysing exit pages helps hotels identify potential issues or bottlenecks in the user journey that may be leading to visitor drop-offs. By improving content or calls-to-action on exit pages, hotels can encourage visitors to explore further or complete the desired conversion action.

Exploring the Key KPIs–Website Traffic, Click Rate & Conversion Rate

Website Traffic

The number of website visitors is a crucial metric as it indicates the effectiveness of your marketing strategies and campaigns in driving traffic to your hotel website. Evaluating this metric helps determine whether your efforts are generating sufficient visibility and engagement.

To assess your performance, consider the following benchmarks for independent and boutique hotels:

- If your website receives 5,000 or more visitors per month, it signifies that you are generating a substantial amount of traffic. This indicates that your marketing strategies are successful in attracting visitors to your website.

- If you receive between 2,500 and 3,500 visitors, you are below the average range. Although you are getting some traffic, there is room for improvement. Consider enhancing your marketing efforts, such as optimising SEO, engaging in targeted advertising, or leveraging social media to increase visibility and drive more traffic to your website.

- If you have fewer than 1,000 visitors, it highlights a critical situation where you urgently need to improve your marketing strategies to boost traffic. A low number of visitors may suggest issues with website visibility, content relevance, or targeting the right audience. Reassess your marketing tactics and explore opportunities for improvement, such as content optimisation, search engine marketing, or partnerships with relevant platforms to attract more visitors to your website.

By monitoring the number of website visitors and comparing it against these benchmarks, you can gain insights into the effectiveness of your marketing efforts. This enables you to identify areas of improvement and take targeted actions to increase traffic, enhance brand visibility, and drive more potential guests to your hotel website.

Click Rate

Click Rate is an important metric that measures the number of visitors who click on the "Book now" button, indicating their interest in initiating the booking process.

Evaluating the Click Rate prompts hoteliers to assess whether their website effectively convinces visitors to start the booking journey. The success of this endeavour is typically influenced by two key factors: the website's user experience (UX) and the design and visuals employed.

A seamless and intuitive UX plays a crucial role in facilitating a smooth and efficient booking process. A well-designed website should prioritise simplicity, ensuring that visitors can easily navigate through the various stages of booking. Additionally, the website's design and visuals should be visually appealing, high-quality and optimised for mobile devices, capturing visitors' attention and enhancing their overall experience.

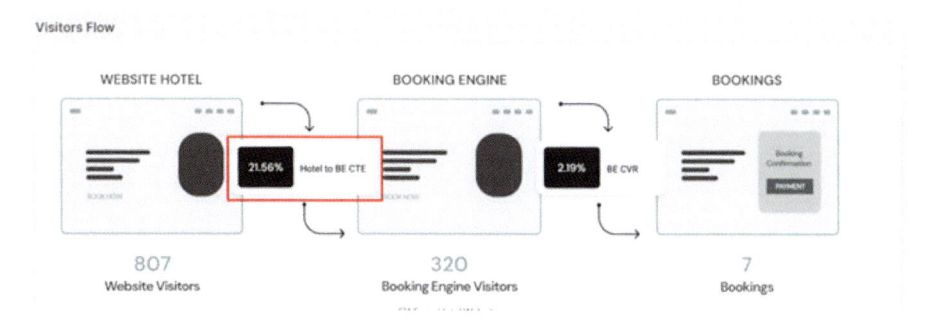

To calculate the Click Rate, you can utilise the following formula: CR = (Booking Engine Visitors / Total Website Visitors) * 100. This data can be obtained from Google Analytics, which provides valuable insights into visitor behaviour and engagement on the website.

Hotel Website to Booking Engine Click Rate

$$\frac{\text{Booking engine visitors}}{\text{Website visitors}} \times 100 = \text{CLICK RATE}$$

To interpret the results, consider the following benchmarks:

- If your CR is 40% or more, your website is doing well.
- If it's between 20% and 30%, you're within the average.
- If it's 10% or less, you should fine-tune your website design, optimise your UX, and display more offers on your website.

< 10% Low   20-30% - Average   > 40% - Good

Conversion Rate

In the hospitality industry, Conversion Rate is a vital metric used to assess the effectiveness of converting website visitors into bookers. There are two types of Conversion Rate to consider:

The first type is the overall Conversion Rate (CVR), which measures the success of your website in converting visitors into bookings. It can be calculated using the formula: CVR = (Total Bookings / Total Website Visitors) * 100. A higher CVR indicates a higher rate of successful conversions and demonstrates the website's effectiveness in driving bookings.

Convertion Rate

$$\frac{\text{Total bookings}}{\text{Total website visitors}} \times 100 = \text{CONVERTION RATE}$$

The second type is the Booking Engine Conversion Rate (BECR), which focuses specifically on the performance of the booking engine in converting visitors into bookings. It can be calculated using the formula: BECR = (Total Bookings / Total Booking Engine Visitors) * 100. This metric helps determine whether the chosen booking engine is effectively converting visitors and may indicate the need to consider alternative providers for better performance.

Booking Engine Conversion Rate

$$\frac{\text{Total bookings}}{\text{Total booking engine visitors}} \times 100 = \text{BOOKING ENGINE CONVERTION RATE}$$

Analysing the BECR is essential as it allows hotels to evaluate the booking engine's key factors that contribute to its success. Factors such as seamless user experience (UX), a simple and intuitive booking process, responsive design for mobile devices, reasonable pricing, personalisation options for brand consistency, rate parity for consistent pricing, flexibility in adjusting room rates based on market conditions, inventory control, booking policies and secure payment options are crucial considerations when assessing the booking engine's performance.

To interpret the results, consider the following benchmarks:

- A CVR percentage of 4% or above indicates a satisfactory level of conversions.
- A CVR between 2% and 3% falls within the average range.
- A CVR of 1% or lower suggests the need to consider switching to a different booking engine provider for improved performance.

< 1% – Low   2-3% – Average   > 4% – Very Good

Regularly analysing and monitoring Conversion Rates can guide hoteliers in making informed decisions about their booking engine provider and implementing strategies to improve conversion rates. By achieving higher Conversion Rates, hotels can enhance their revenue potential and increase the overall success of their online booking processes.

Your Website Analytics Check List

Hotel website checklist:

- **User experience:** Make sure that your website navigation is simple and that you have a clear call to action. Use a familiar call to action such as "Book Now" or "Make a Reservation". Make sure that your booking widget is easily visible, the best price guarantee is highlighted and the special offers are easy to find.
- **Offers:** Highlight the offers most likely to be attractive to your audience. You need to clearly highlight your special offers and personalise them as much as possible. For example, show your Early

Bird offer to the markets which have a long lead period and the last-minute offer to the short-haul market. Add a bit of urgency by displaying a flash sale offer available for a limited time.

- **Website loading time:** Make sure that your website loads fast enough on both desktop and mobile devices. Every second counts. A one-second delay in page response can result in a 7% reduction in conversions.
- **Website traffic quality:** It's important to see if your marketing campaigns are bringing traffic to your website from the right markets. Target the markets that historically book the most on your website and have high conversion rates.

Booking engine conversion rate checklist:

- **Booking engine navigation issue:** A good practice is to make the booking process as simple as possible and reduce the booking steps to 2 or 3 at most.
- **Rates and offers:** It's important to make it as easy as possible for users to book, so don't overwhelm them with too many options. Provide only 1-2 rates per room type.
- **Availability:** If most of your inventory is not available it would be harder for the users to make a booking and the conversion rates would immediately drop.
- **Cancellation policies:** A good practice is also to offer flexible cancellation policies. Our experience shows that hotels with flexible cancellation policies tend to have much higher conversion rates.
- **Vendor:** Lastly, choose a vendor that consistently delivers high conversion rates for all their properties.

The Relationship between Website Analytics and Revenue Management Strategies:

Website analytics and revenue management strategies are closely interconnected.

The data obtained from website analytics directly influences revenue management decisions. Here's how website analytics contributes to revenue management strategies:

> **Pricing Optimisation:** By analysing website traffic, conversion rates, and user behaviour, hotels can understand which marketing efforts drive the most valuable traffic and conversions. This information allows revenue managers to adjust pricing strategies based on demand generated by various marketing channels and campaigns. For example, during periods of high website traffic from paid advertising, revenue managers may consider implementing dynamic pricing to capitalise on increased interest and drive revenue.

> **Inventory Management:** Website analytics provide insights into peak booking periods and demand fluctuations. With this information, revenue managers can optimise room inventory and allocate available rooms strategically to meet demand. During high-demand periods identified through website analytics, revenue managers may limit room availability on external channels and focus on driving more direct bookings to maximise revenue.

> **Personalisation and Targeting:** Website analytics help hotels identify user segments with different preferences and behaviours. Revenue managers can use this data to create personalised offers, packages and promotions for specific customer groups, enhancing the likelihood of conversion and revenue generation.

> **Performance Measurement:** Website analytics serves as a critical tool for measuring the effectiveness of revenue management strategies. By tracking key metrics such as conversion rate and revenue

generated, revenue managers can evaluate the impact of their pricing and inventory decisions and make data-driven adjustments for continuous improvement.

In conclusion, the key metrics obtained from website analytics play a vital role in revenue management strategies for hotels.

By understanding website traffic patterns, conversion rates and user behaviour, hotels can optimise pricing, inventory management, and marketing efforts to drive direct bookings and increase revenue.

The data-driven insights obtained through website analytics empower revenue managers to make informed decisions that enhance the hotel's online presence, user experience and overall profitability.

In this section, we delved into the essential components of analysing website performance and its crucial role in optimising revenue and marketing strategies. You've learned how website analytics provide valuable insights into user behaviour, enabling hotels to tailor their websites to better serve guest needs, enhance the user experience and drive direct bookings.

Your newfound knowledge equips you to not only enhance the user experience but also to chart a course towards the ultimate destination: driving direct bookings. As you venture forth, keep in mind that website analytics aren't just a tool; it's the lantern that illuminates your path to success in the dynamic world of hospitality.

With the skills and insights gained in this chapter, you're poised to make data-driven decisions that will set your hotel apart, offering an experience that not only meets but exceeds guest expectations. So, take these lessons to heart as you step confidently into the next phase of your journey, armed with the wisdom of website analytics as your guiding star.

Chapter 1: Key Takeaways

Here is a summary of the key takeaways from Chapter 1:

1. **Homepage Impact**: Design a captivating homepage with high-quality visuals and a strong headline that conveys your hotel's unique value proposition to make a lasting impression on visitors.

2. **User-Friendly Navigation**: Intuitive and easy-to-use navigation with well-organised menu items and dropdowns helps visitors find information quickly. Ensure each page includes a visible booking button for a seamless booking process.

3. **Website Speed Matters**: Optimise website speed by compressing images and using caching techniques to reduce page loading times. Slow websites can discourage visitors from staying and booking.

4. **Visual Content Engagement**: Engage potential guests with high-quality images and videos showcasing your hotel's rooms, amenities, dining options and local attractions, creating an immersive experience.

5. **Mobile Responsiveness:** Ensure your website is responsive across various screen sizes, especially for mobile devices, as an increasing number of users browse on smartphones and tablets.

6. **Clear CTAs**: Implement clear and strategically placed Calls-to-Action (CTAs) that guide visitors towards desired actions like booking rooms or signing up for newsletters, using attention-grabbing language and contrasting colours.

7. **Simple Booking Process**: Streamline the booking process with a user-friendly form, clear instructions and secure payment options to minimise friction and encourage more direct bookings.

8. **Value of Website Analytics**: Website analytics provides insights into customer data, booking patterns and user behaviour, enabling the identification of revenue opportunities, customer segments and demand patterns.

9. **Revenue-Marketing Intersection**: RevMarketing uses website analytics to pinpoint touchpoints where revenue objectives and marketing strategies intersect, bridging the gap between revenue goals and marketing efforts.
10. **User Behaviour Insights**: Website analytics helps hotels understand user behaviour, such as browsing patterns, clicked elements and preferred offers, allowing for tailored website improvements.
11. **User Experience Optimisation**: Analysing website analytics aids in identifying usability issues and optimising design for a seamless user experience, leading to increased engagement and direct bookings.
12. **Key Metrics Overview**: Key metrics include website traffic, conversion rate, bounce rate, average session duration, source of traffic and exit pages, which collectively provide a comprehensive picture of website performance.
13. **Click Rate Significance**: Click Rate measures the number of visitors clicking on booking buttons, indicating website persuasiveness and UX quality for initiating bookings.
14. **Conversion Rate Assessment**: The Conversion Rate, both overall and for the booking engine, indicates the website's success in converting visitors to bookings, helping evaluate booking engine performance and identify improvement areas.

2

Understanding Your Guests' Booking Behaviour

Welcome to this enlightening chapter where we embark on an exploration of booking behaviour, a critical pillar in the hospitality industry's foundation. Here, we embark on a journey to unravel the intricate factors that steer booking decisions from the timing of reservations to the various channels through which they are initiated. We'll uncover the myriad of considerations that converge to shape the ultimate choice.

Within the confines of this section, you'll be armed with the tools necessary to navigate the labyrinth of booking behaviour with precision. By peering into the minds of travellers, meticulously examining their booking patterns and dissecting their decisions, you'll acquire a treasure trove of invaluable insights.

These insights, in turn, will become your compass in optimising revenue strategies and refining marketing efforts. Most importantly, they will empower you to provide guests with the seamless and delightful booking experiences they truly deserve. So, let's embark on this journey of discovery, where the art of understanding leads to the science of success in the world of hospitality.

Why is Booking Behaviour Imprortant?

What is booking behaviour?

Booking behavior refers to the actions, preferences, and decision-making patterns displayed by travelers when reserving accommodation. It encompasses a wide range of factors, including the channels through which bookings are made, the timing of reservations, the duration of stays, and the considerations that influence the final choice.

For hoteliers and those involved in the hospitality industry, understanding booking behaviour is crucial for optimising revenue, enhancing guest experiences and staying ahead of the competition.

Why is booking behaviour important?
An in-depth understanding of booking behaviour allows hoteliers to predict and anticipate demand patterns accurately. By analysing historical booking data, hotel managers can identify trends and plan their marketing and operational strategies accordingly. This predictive capability is particularly crucial during peak seasons or special events when demand is high, enabling hotels to optimise pricing, availability and resources to maximise revenue.

Each traveller is unique, and their preferences can significantly impact their booking decisions.

> By segmenting customers based on their booking behavior, hotels can create targeted marketing campaigns and offer personalized promotions.

This personalised approach enhances customer satisfaction and encourages repeat bookings, fostering long-term loyalty.

The travel industry is dynamic, with booking behaviour continually evolving due to technological advancements, shifting traveller preferences and external events. By staying attuned to these changes, **hoteliers can adapt their marketing strategies and offerings to meet new demands effectively**. Being proactive in understanding booking behaviour ensures that hotels remain competitive and relevant in the ever-changing marketplace.

Effective revenue management relies heavily on understanding booking behaviour. By studying historical booking data, hotels can implement dynamic pricing strategies, adjust room rates based on demand fluctuations, and optimise inventory distribution across various booking channels. This data-driven approach maximises revenue potential while maintaining price competitiveness.

Key Booking Behaviour Analysis

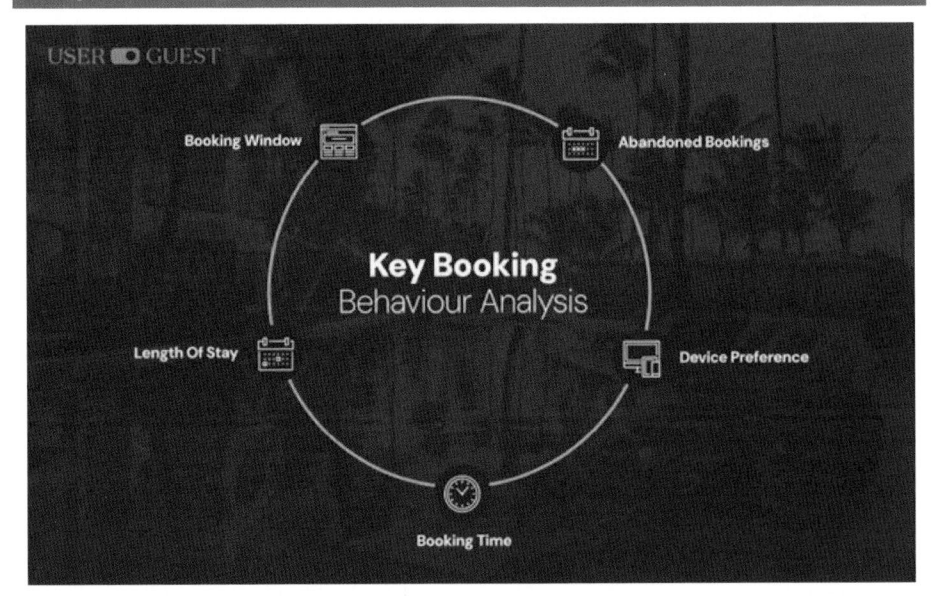

Understanding booking behaviour is of utmost importance for hoteliers as it provides valuable insights into the preferences and decision-making processes of potential guests.

Analysing booking behaviour allows hoteliers to identify patterns and trends in customer preferences, such as preferred room types, booking lead times, preferred length of stay and other factors that influence decision-making. This knowledge enables them to tailor their marketing efforts and pricing strategies to effectively target and attract their desired audience.

Booking Window:
The booking window refers to the time period between the date a guest makes a reservation and the actual stay at the hotel. Analysing booking windows provides valuable insights into guests' planning habits and decision-making processes. Some guests prefer to book well in advance while others may book closer to their travel dates. Understanding these patterns allows hotels to implement dynamic pricing strategies effectively.

- Early Bookers: Guests who book well in advance may be enticed by early-bird discounts or other promotional offers. By identifying this segment, hotels can launch special deals to attract these planners and secure bookings early, helping with cash flow and revenue forecasting.
- Last-Minute Bookers: Some guests prefer to book at the last moment due to spontaneous travel plans or uncertainty. Hotels can offer last-minute deals or flash sales to target these customers and fill up any remaining inventory.

Length of Stay:
Analysing the typical length of guest stays helps hotels optimise their revenue management strategies. Different lengths of stay can impact pricing, resource allocation and overall guest satisfaction.

- Short Stays: Guests who stay for short durations may prioritise convenience and may not be as price-sensitive. Hotels can create packages or add-ons tailored to these guests, enhancing their experience and increasing ancillary revenue.
- Extended Stays: Guests staying for longer periods may seek value-for-money deals and extended-stay discounts. By understanding this segment, hotels can offer extended stay packages, providing a competitive edge and ensuring guest loyalty.

Booking Time:
Analysing the time of day or day of the week when most direct bookings occur helps hotels optimise their marketing efforts and improve customer support availability during peak booking periods.

- Peak Booking Hours: Identifying the peak hours when guests make direct bookings allows hotels to schedule targeted marketing campaigns and personalised offers during these periods, increasing conversion rates.

- Support Availability: Understanding the peak booking times also helps hotels allocate customer support resources efficiently, ensuring that guests receive timely assistance during critical moments.

Device Preference:
As technology evolves, guests have various devices at their disposal to make reservations. Identifying guests' device preferences is crucial for ensuring a seamless booking experience.

- Mobile Users: If a significant portion of bookings come from mobile devices, hotels must ensure that their website is mobile-friendly and offers a smooth, easy-to-navigate interface.
- Desktop Users: For guests who prefer booking through desktop computers, the hotel's website should be optimised for larger screens, ensuring a visually appealing and user-friendly experience.
- Tablet Users: Understanding tablet usage for bookings allows hotels to customise the booking process for this specific segment, maximising conversion rates.

Abandoned Bookings:
Monitoring and understanding the reasons behind booking abandonments on the direct channel is essential for improving conversion rates and reducing lost revenue opportunities.

- Streamlining the Booking Process: If guests frequently abandon bookings at a specific stage, hotels can optimise that stage to reduce friction and simplify the process, increasing the likelihood of completing the reservation.
- Addressing Pain Points: Identifying common reasons for abandonment, such as high prices, complicated forms, or technical issues, allows hotels to address these concerns and improve the overall booking experience.

Identifying Touchpoints and Optimising User Experience

Identifying touchpoints is crucial for understanding where guests interact with your hotel throughout their booking journey. These touchpoints can include your website, social media channels, booking platforms, email communications and on-site experiences.

- **Website Optimisation**: Your hotel's website is a central touchpoint for potential guests. Optimising its design, navigation and content ensures a user-friendly experience that encourages bookings.
- **Seamless Booking Platforms**: If you use third-party booking platforms, ensure that the integration is seamless and provides a consistent user experience.
- **Personalisation**: Utilise data and guest preferences to personalise interactions and recommendations, providing guests with a tailored experience that meets their needs and preferences.
- **Responsive Customer Support**: Offer timely and responsive customer support through various channels, such as live chat, email or phone, to address inquiries promptly.

In the fiercely competitive landscape of the hospitality industry, delving deep into the nuances of key booking behaviours becomes a priceless asset for hoteliers. It's the compass guiding them toward revenue optimisation, elevated guest experiences and maintaining a competitive edge in the field.

As hoteliers decode the intricacies of the booking window, length of stay, booking timing, device preferences and even abandoned bookings, they unveil a treasure trove of insights. These insights, in turn, serve as the foundation for tailoring marketing strategies, pricing models and user experiences to align with guest expectations.

In this data-driven journey, the goal is not just to meet but to exceed these expectations, fostering guest loyalty that transcends a single stay. It's the key to sustaining that all-important competitive edge in the dynamic and ever-evolving world of hospitality, where staying ahead of the curve is the hallmark of success.

Personalisation through Booking Behaviour Analysis

In this section, we embark on a journey to unlock the potential of booking behaviour data for the art of personalisation. Here, we'll delve into the myriad of ways through which this data can be harnessed to ensure that every guest is not just welcomed but valued and appreciated throughout their stay.

What is Personalisation?

What Is Personalisation?

Personalisation is a powerful tool in the hospitality industry, allowing hotels to create unique and tailored experiences for their guests. By leveraging insights gained from booking behavior analysis, hoteliers can implement personalised strategies that cater to individual preferences and enhance overall guest satisfaction.

Understanding Guest Segmentation:

Segmenting guests based on their booking behaviour is the foundation of effective personalisation.

By categorising guests into different groups, such as business travellers, families, solo travellers or frequent visitors, hotels can offer customised services and experiences that align with their specific needs and preferences. Understanding guest segments allows for more targeted marketing campaigns and personalised offers, maximising the chances of conversion and guest loyalty.

Personalising Communication:
Using booking behaviour data, hotels can personalise communication with guests before, during and after their stay.

Tailoring pre-arrival emails or messages based on guest preferences and past interactions demonstrates attention to detail and enhances the overall guest experience. During the stay, offering personalised recommendations for nearby attractions or dining options adds value and creates a memorable experience for guests. Post-stay follow-up emails or surveys based on the guest's stay preferences provide an opportunity to gather feedback and encourage future bookings.

Personalised Loyalty Programs:
Loyalty programs play a significant role in guest retention and repeat bookings. By analysing booking behaviour, hotels can identify loyal guests and reward them with personalised loyalty programs. Tailored incentives, such as exclusive discounts, room upgrades or complimentary amenities, demonstrate appreciation for their loyalty, encouraging continued patronage and advocacy.

Customised Packages and Offers:
Guests have diverse preferences when it comes to travel experiences. Analysing booking behaviour enables hotels to create personalised packages and offers that cater to specific guest interests. For example, offering adventure packages for thrill-seekers, relaxation packages for spa enthusiasts or family packages with child-friendly activities can attract guests seeking tailored experiences.

Personalisation through booking behaviour analysis is a key driver of guest satisfaction and loyalty in the hospitality industry. Understanding guest preferences, needs, and behaviours allows hotels to offer tailored experiences, personalised communication and unique packages that resonate with individual guests.

By leveraging booking behaviour data, hoteliers can create memorable stays, encourage repeat bookings and build strong guest relationships, ultimately leading to enhanced revenue and a distinguished reputation in the competitive market.

Embrace the power of personalisation to exceed guest expectations and deliver unforgettable experiences at your hotel.

Personalising the Experience: Practical Tips

Personalising the user experience on the hotel's direct booking channel, particularly the website, is a crucial aspect of enhancing guest satisfaction and increasing conversions. By tailoring the booking process to meet individual guest needs, hotels can create a seamless and compelling booking experience that fosters loyalty and positive reviews.

The Right Dates:
Presenting the right dates to guests is essential for a smooth booking experience. Utilising intelligent booking engines that showcase real-time availability and pricing allows guests to easily find the dates that align with their travel plans. This feature eliminates the frustration of searching for availability and ensures that guests can quickly secure their desired dates.

> **USER ⊙ GUEST**
>
> Matching the user's booking intent to the hotel's inventory needs is crucial for successful RevMarketing. By understanding when guests are most likely to book, hotels can optimize their pricing and availability strategies, ensuring that they are offering competitive rates during peak booking periods.

The Right Room Category:

Personalising the room category selection is a powerful way to enhance the guest experience. By analysing guest preferences and booking history, hotels can offer room recommendations or highlight specific categories that align with the guest's needs and preferences. For example, if a guest has a history of booking deluxe rooms with a pool view, the website can showcase these options prominently, making it easier for the guest to find their preferred room category.

The Right Moment to Convince:

Understanding guests' booking behaviour and identifying the right moment to convince them to book directly is crucial. Implementing strategic pop-ups, targeted messaging, or personalised offers during the guest's browsing journey can create a sense of urgency or exclusivity.

For instance, if a guest has been browsing the website for a specific date and room category but hasn't initiated the booking process, a pop-up with a limited-time promotion or a special discount for direct bookings can encourage them to make the decision to book immediately.

The Right Offer:
Delivering the right offer is a key element in enticing guests to choose the direct booking channel. This involves providing exclusive benefits and types of offers that align with the user's booking behaviour and preferences.

For example, if a guest is a member of the hotel's loyalty program, the website can display personalised offers or special perks for loyalty members. By clearly communicating the unique value proposition of booking directly on the hotel website, such as complimentary breakfast, free Wi-Fi or room upgrades, hotels can motivate guests to forego third-party booking platforms and take advantage of the added benefits available through direct bookings.

Personalising the user experience on the hotel's direct booking channel is a strategic approach to enhance guest satisfaction and increase conversions. By delivering the right dates, room categories, moments to convince, and offers that align with guests' preferences and booking behaviour, hotels can create a tailored and compelling booking experience. This personalised approach not only fosters guest loyalty but also drives more direct bookings, reducing dependence on third-party booking platforms and enhancing the hotel's revenue and reputation in the highly competitive hospitality industry.

Throughout this chapter, you've delved into the intricate craft of tailoring guest experiences through the prism of booking behaviour insights. From the mastery of guest segmentation and the artistry of personalised communication to the finesse of crafting customised packages and the seamless enhancement of the booking process, you've woven together a comprehensive tapestry of personalisation.

In your journey, you've grasped the essence of how personalisation becomes the catalyst for elevated guest satisfaction and unwavering loyalty. With these practical strategies at your disposal, you're now equipped to embark on a path where every stay becomes unforgettable, where guest relationships flourish and where you not only survive but thrive in the competitive landscape of the hospitality market. Your arsenal of knowledge and expertise is the key to unlocking new heights in guest service and hotel success.

Chapter 2: Key Takeaways

Here are the most important key takeaways from Chapter 2:

Understanding Booking Behaviour

1. Insights for Optimisation: Understanding booking behaviour provides insights into guest preferences, enabling effective marketing and pricing strategies to attract the desired audience.

2. Booking Patterns: Analysing booking windows, length of stay, and booking times help hotels adapt strategies for different guest preferences and planning habits.

3. Device Influence: Recognising device preferences (mobile, desktop, tablet) ensures a seamless booking experience across various platforms.

4. Abandoned Bookings: Addressing common reasons for booking abandonment improves conversion rates by simplifying and streamlining the booking process.

5. Guest Interaction: Identifying touchpoints (website, social media, emails) aids in optimising user experiences throughout the booking journey.

Personalisation through Booking Behaviour Analysis

6. Segmentation Strategies: Guest segmentation based on behaviour enhances personalisation, enabling tailored marketing campaigns and experiences.

7. Customised Communication: Personalising pre-arrival, during-stay and post-stay communication improves guest experience and fosters loyalty.
8. Loyalty Programs: Tailored loyalty programs, based on booking behaviour, reward loyal guests and encourage repeat bookings.
9. Tailored Packages: Creating customised packages based on guest interests enhances the attractiveness of direct bookings.
10. Direct Booking Personalisation: Personalising the booking experience through strategic date presentation, room category suggestions, timely offers and special incentives fosters guest loyalty, drives conversions and elevates revenue potential.

By mastering these key takeaways, you'll be equipped to navigate the complexities of booking behaviour and leverage personalised strategies to enhance guest satisfaction, loyalty and revenue in the dynamic hospitality industry.

3

Revenue Management Fundamentals

Within the pages of this chapter, we embark on a journey through the core principles and dynamic strategies of revenue management, an integral component of our mission to supercharge hotel profitability.

Our destination: a realm where RevMarketing principles intersect with revenue management and creates a synergy that elevates your hotel's financial performance.

As we explore the intricacies of revenue management, we'll unveil the secrets behind understanding these principles, deciphering market demand dynamics and implementing dynamic pricing strategies. These invaluable tools will empower you to navigate the intricate web of data, enabling you to make informed, data-driven decisions that propel your hotel toward maximum profitability.

So, fasten your seatbelts as we delve into the world of RevMarketing-powered revenue management, where strategic insights and dynamic strategies converge to unlock the full potential of your hotel's financial success.

Understanding Revenue Management Principles and Pricing Strategies

What is Revenue Management?

Revenue management, often referred to as yield management, is a sophisticated and strategic approach that hotels employ to meticulously optimise their room rates and inventory allocation to maximise revenue and profitability. This practice requires a comprehensive understanding of market dynamics, customer behaviour and competitor actions to make informed decisions that impact the hotel's bottom line.

At its core, revenue management involves analysing a multitude of data points and variables to dynamically adjust room rates and availability. This is done in response to fluctuations in market demand, seasonal patterns, special events and even day-to-day changes in booking behaviour. By utilising advanced forecasting techniques and leveraging historical data, hotels can make precise decisions on when to raise or lower room rates and how to allocate rooms across various booking channels.

The primary objective of revenue management is to achieve optimal occupancy levels while maximising revenue per available room (RevPAR). Achieving this delicate balance requires not only a deep understanding of pricing dynamics but also a keen awareness of customer segmentation and their willingness to pay. By segmenting customers into different groups based on factors such as booking behaviour, demographics and preferences, hotels can tailor their pricing strategies to effectively target each segment.

One of the key challenges in revenue management is identifying the most profitable mix of business. This entails deciding which guests to prioritise during peak periods and how to incentivise different customer segments to book during slower periods. Revenue management also involves strategic decisions about overbooking, which involves accepting more reservations than available rooms to account for potential cancellations or no-shows.

Modern revenue management is heavily reliant on technology and data analytics. Hotels use sophisticated revenue management systems that integrate data from various sources, including booking engines, property management systems and external market data. These systems utilise complex algorithms to provide real-time insights and recommendations to revenue managers, allowing them to make informed decisions swiftly.

Ultimately, the successful implementation of revenue management strategies can lead to substantial increases in revenue and profitability for hotels. By continuously adapting to changing market conditions and customer behaviour, hotels can ensure they are selling their rooms at the optimal price points to the most relevant customer segments. This approach not only enhances the hotel's financial performance but also contributes to a more efficient and sustainable operation within the competitive landscape of the hospitality industry.

Pricing Strategies in Revenue Management

In revenue management, pricing strategies play a pivotal role in maximising hotel revenue and profitability. Different pricing approaches are employed to ensure that room rates are set optimally to align with market demand, customer behaviour and competitive positioning. Let's delve deeper into the key pricing strategies utilised in revenue management.

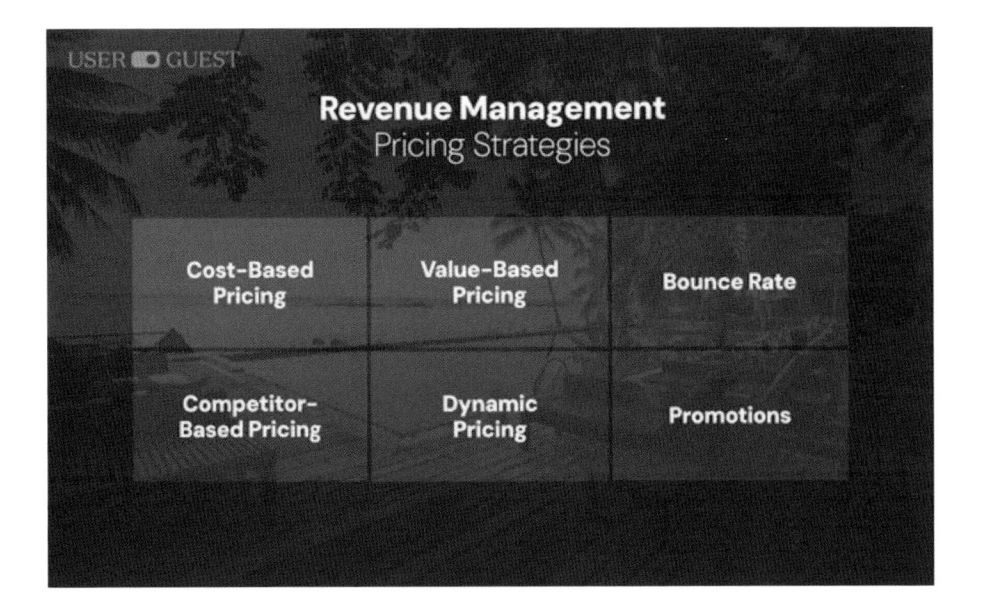

Revenue Management Pricing Strategies

Cost-Based Pricing	Value-Based Pricing	Bounce Rate
Competitor-Based Pricing	Dynamic Pricing	Promotions

Cost-Based Pricing:

Cost-based pricing is a straightforward method where room rates are determined by considering the hotel's operational costs and desired profit margin.

Hoteliers calculate all the expenses associated with running the property, including staff salaries, utilities, maintenance and other overhead costs. They then add a desired profit margin on top of the total costs to arrive at the room rate.

While cost-based pricing ensures that expenses are covered, it may not consider factors like demand fluctuations or competitor pricing, potentially leading to missed revenue opportunities.

Value-Based Pricing:

Value-based pricing revolves around the concept of determining room rates based on the perceived value of the hotel's offerings from the customer's perspective.

This approach focuses on understanding what features and amenities guests consider valuable and are willing to pay a premium for.

For example, a hotel with exceptional customer service, luxurious amenities and a prime location may set higher room rates based on the perceived added value it provides to guests.

Value-based pricing allows hotels to capitalise on their unique selling points and create a premium brand image, attracting customers who prioritise quality and experience over price.

Competitor-Based Pricing:

Competitor-based pricing involves analysing the pricing strategies of rival hotels within the same market or geographic area.

By monitoring competitor rates, hoteliers can position their room rates strategically to remain competitive. If a hotel's offerings and amenities are similar to those of its competitors, it may choose to price rooms in line with the prevailing market rates.

On the other hand, if a hotel offers unique and differentiated services, it may price above competitors, emphasising the additional value it provides to guests. Competitor-based pricing requires ongoing monitoring of the competitive landscape to adjust room rates as needed.

Dynamic Pricing:

Dynamic pricing is a fundamental aspect of revenue management. It involves adjusting room rates in real time based on changes in market demand, booking trends and other external factors.

By leveraging data analytics and forecasting models, hotels can dynamically set room rates to optimise revenue. For instance, during periods of high demand, such as peak travel seasons or special events, room rates may be increased to capitalise on increased interest.

Conversely, during low-demand periods, hotels may offer promotional rates or discounts to stimulate demand and fill rooms. Dynamic pricing ensures that room rates are aligned with demand fluctuations, resulting in improved revenue performance.

Discount Strategies and Promotions:
Discount strategies and promotions are used strategically to stimulate demand and attract specific customer segments. Hotels may offer early booking discounts, last-minute deals or seasonal promotions to entice guests to make reservations. Additionally, loyalty programs and special offers targeting repeat guests can enhance guest retention and drive direct bookings. Careful consideration of the timing and duration of promotions is essential to avoid excessive discounting that could erode profitability.

Implementing a balanced pricing strategy that incorporates elements of value-based pricing, competitor analysis and dynamic pricing is critical for revenue management success. By continuously monitoring market trends, guest preferences and competitor actions, hoteliers can adjust room rates strategically to optimise revenue while delivering compelling value to guests.

The Revenue Management Cycle

The revenue management cycle is a continuous process that revenue managers follow to optimise room rates, manage inventory and maximise hotel revenue and profitability. It involves several interconnected stages, each contributing to the overall success of revenue management strategies. Let's explore the key elements of the revenue management cycle in more detail:

Forecasting:
The revenue management cycle begins with forecasting, a critical step in predicting future demand for hotel rooms. Revenue managers analyse

historical booking data, market trends, seasonality and other relevant factors to generate demand forecasts for different periods, such as daily, weekly or monthly. These forecasts serve as the foundation for revenue management decisions throughout the cycle.

Effective forecasting requires the use of advanced data analytics tools and demand forecasting models. Revenue managers must accurately anticipate variations in demand due to seasonal patterns, special events, holidays or other factors that may influence booking behaviour.

Pricing:

Based on demand forecasts, revenue managers develop pricing strategies to optimise room rates. The goal is to set rates at levels that align with market demand and maximise revenue. Pricing decisions consider factors such as demand fluctuations, competitor pricing and customer preferences.

Pricing strategies may involve different rate categories with varying restrictions, promotional offers and dynamic pricing. Revenue managers use a combination of data analytics, competitive analysis and revenue management systems to arrive at the most effective pricing decisions.

Inventory Management:

Inventory management is crucial for effectively managing the availability of room types and rates. Revenue managers strategically allocate room inventory to different booking channels, such as the hotel's website, online travel agencies (OTAs) and global distribution systems (GDS). The goal is to achieve optimal distribution across channels while minimising the risk of overbooking or underselling rooms.

Effective inventory management also involves rate fences, which are conditions or restrictions applied to specific rate categories. Rate fences ensure that certain rates are offered only to specific customer segments or under specific booking conditions. For example, non-refundable rates may be offered for guests booking in advance, while flexible rates may be available for last-minute bookings.

Evaluation:

The evaluation stage is a critical component of the revenue management cycle, where revenue managers assess the performance of their pricing and inventory management strategies. Key performance indicators (KPIs) are used to measure the effectiveness of revenue management efforts.

Common revenue management KPIs include Revenue Per Available Room (RevPAR), Average Daily Rate (ADR) and Occupancy Rate. These metrics help revenue managers track revenue performance, occupancy levels and pricing effectiveness. By comparing actual performance against forecasted results, revenue managers can identify areas for improvement and make data-driven adjustments to their strategies.

Data analytics and reporting tools are utilised in the evaluation stage to generate comprehensive reports that showcase revenue trends, demand patterns and revenue KPIs. These reports provide valuable insights into the effectiveness of revenue management efforts and serve as a basis for future decision-making.

The revenue management cycle is an iterative process, meaning that revenue managers continually repeat these stages to adjust their strategies based on changing market conditions and performance feedback. By continuously analysing market trends, guest behaviour and competitor actions, revenue managers can optimise pricing decisions and inventory management to achieve maximum revenue and profitability for the hotel.

Market Segmentation and Demand Analysis

Market segmentation and demand analysis are critical components of revenue management, as they provide valuable insights into guest preferences, booking behaviour and market trends. By understanding different customer segments and their specific demands, hotels can tailor pricing strategies and marketing efforts to optimise revenue and cater to the needs of various guest groups. Let's delve into the details of market segmentation and demand analysis.

Market Segmentation:

Market segmentation involves dividing the overall market into distinct groups of customers with similar characteristics, needs and preferences. The goal of segmentation is to identify and understand the unique demands of different customer segments to create targeted marketing strategies and pricing approaches. Here are some common market segmentation criteria used in the hotel industry:

a. Demographic Segmentation: Segmenting customers based on demographic factors such as age, gender, income and family size. Different demographic groups may have different travel preferences and spending habits.

b. Geographic Segmentation: Dividing customers based on geographic locations such as country, region or city. Geographic segmentation helps identify the primary source markets for the hotel and adjust marketing efforts accordingly.

c. Psychographic Segmentation: Segmenting customers based on their lifestyle, interests, values and attitudes. This segmentation allows hotels to cater to guests with specific preferences or travel motivations.

d. Behavioural Segmentation: Dividing customers based on their past behaviours such as booking frequency, length of stay and preferred room types. Behavioural segmentation helps identify loyal customers and design targeted loyalty programs.

e. Socioeconomic Segmentation: Segmenting customers based on their social class or occupation. Socioeconomic segmentation may influence spending patterns and accommodation preferences.

Demand Analysis:

Demand analysis involves studying historical booking data and analysing patterns and trends in customer demand. By understanding demand fluctuations, hotels can anticipate periods of high and low demand, enabling them to adjust pricing and inventory management strategies accordingly. Here are the key elements of demand analysis:

a. Historical Booking Data: Revenue managers analyse historical booking data to identify booking patterns, seasonality and demand trends. This data provides insights into past performance and helps forecast future demand.

b. Seasonal Demand Variations: Demand analysis identifies seasonal peaks and valleys in booking patterns. Seasonal demand variations may be influenced by holidays, local events, weather conditions or traditional travel periods.

c. Special Events and Conferences: Hotels examine the impact of special events, conferences and festivals on demand. Such events can lead to a surge in room bookings, warranting strategic pricing adjustments.

d. Length of Stay Analysis: Understanding the average length of stay for different customer segments allows hotels to optimise room availability and tailor pricing for short and extended stays.

e. Advance Booking Patterns: Analysing the lead time between bookings and the actual stay dates helps hotels assess booking pace and adjust pricing strategies for advance bookings and last-minute reservations.

f. Booking Window Analysis: Analysing the time between the booking date and the stay date to understand guest booking behaviour. This information helps in setting promotional rates and managing inventory effectively.

By combining market segmentation and demand analysis, hotels can develop targeted marketing campaigns, set strategic room rates and optimise inventory management. Revenue managers can identify the most profitable customer segments, forecast demand with greater accuracy and implement dynamic pricing strategies to maximise revenue during periods of high demand while driving demand during low-demand periods. The insights gained from market segmentation and demand analysis enable hotels to make data-driven decisions that align with customer preferences and market conditions, leading to improved revenue performance and guest satisfaction.

Dynamic Pricing and Revenue Management Systems

Dynamic Pricing Strategies: Dynamic pricing is a fundamental aspect of revenue management. By analysing real-time data on market demand, competitor rates and booking trends, hotels can adjust room rates dynamically to optimise revenue. Revenue management software and tools automate this process, allowing hotels to respond quickly to changes in market conditions and adjust prices accordingly.

Revenue Management Systems: Implementing an efficient revenue management system is crucial for effective revenue management. Revenue management systems integrate data analytics and forecasting models to generate demand forecasts and recommend optimal room rates. These systems help hoteliers make informed pricing decisions and automate the process of adjusting room rates across various distribution channels.

Measuring and Evaluating Revenue Performance: To assess the success of revenue management strategies, hotels must monitor key performance indicators (KPIs) related to revenue and profitability. Common KPIs include Revenue Per Available Room (RevPAR), Average Daily Rate (ADR) and Occupancy Rate. Post-implementation evaluations enable hotels to measure the impact of revenue management strategies and identify areas for improvement. By continually analysing performance metrics and making data-driven adjustments, hotels can optimise revenue and profitability.

Chapter 3: Key Takeaways

Here are the 10 most important takeaways from Chapter 3: Revenue Management Fundamentals:

1. Revenue Management Definition: Revenue management is a strategic approach that hotels use to optimise room rates and inventory, dynamically adjusting prices based on market demand, customer behaviour, and competitor pricing to maximise revenue and profitability.

2. Pricing Strategies: Hotels employ various pricing strategies, including cost-based pricing, value-based pricing, competitor-based pricing and dynamic pricing to set optimal room rates that cater to different market conditions and customer preferences.

3. Dynamic Pricing: Dynamic pricing is a cornerstone of revenue management, involving real-time adjustments of room rates in response to changes in market demand and competitive landscape, ensuring rates remain competitive and revenue is maximised.

4. Inventory Management: Effective inventory management involves strategically allocating room inventory across different booking channels while considering rate fences, restrictions and segmentation to avoid overbooking or underselling rooms.

5. Revenue Management Cycle: The revenue management cycle is an ongoing process that includes forecasting demand, setting prices, managing inventory and evaluating performance. It is a continuous loop of data-driven decision-making to optimise revenue.

6. Forecasting: Forecasting entails predicting future demand by analysing historical booking data, market trends, and relevant factors, providing a foundation for pricing and inventory decisions.

7. Pricing Decisions: Revenue managers determine pricing strategies based on demand forecasts, competitor rates and other factors to set optimal room rates that maximise revenue.

8. Demand Analysis: Understanding historical booking patterns, seasonal trends, length of stay and booking windows helps revenue managers anticipate demand fluctuations and adjust strategies accordingly.
9. Market Segmentation: Market segmentation involves dividing customers into distinct groups based on characteristics like demographics, geography, psychographics, behaviour and socioeconomic factors. This segmentation informs targeted marketing and pricing strategies.
10. Dynamic Pricing Strategies: Utilising real-time data, dynamic pricing strategies adjust room rates based on market demand, competitor rates and booking trends. Revenue management systems automate this process, enabling swift response to changes.

By mastering these takeaways, you'll be well-equipped to apply revenue management principles, analyse market demand, implement dynamic pricing and make data-driven decisions to maximise profitability for your hotel.

Conclusion

As we draw the curtains on Chapter 3, we commend you for your dedication and successful navigation of the intricate terrain of revenue management. You now possess a robust foundation in revenue management fundamentals, encompassing pricing strategies, demand analysis and the art of implementing dynamic pricing to unlock the full potential of your hotel's profitability.

With these insights firmly in your grasp, you stand at the helm of informed decision-making. You have the power to fine-tune room rates, maximise revenue streams and steer your hotel toward a future of financial prosperity. Your journey is a testament to the RevMarketing approach where mastery of revenue management principles becomes the key to unlocking unparalleled success in the competitive world of hospitality.

4

Practical Strategies to Drive Incremental Revenue Through the Hotel Website

Within the realm of hotel revenue management, one of the most potent tools at your disposal is your hotel's website. In this chapter, we'll delve into the boundless potential it holds as your most lucrative segment, a realm where the rules are different, and the rewards are substantial.

Unlike bookings channelled through online travel agencies (OTAs), direct bookings via your hotel's website come with a distinct advantage: no commission fees. This means your hotel retains a more substantial slice of the revenue pie. These savings are not mere numbers; they are your passport to enhancing guest experiences and offering added value and benefits that set your hotel apart.

Furthermore, when guests choose to book directly through your hotel's website, a direct line of communication is established. The coveted email addresses you acquire open doors to a world of possibilities. It's the portal for remarketing initiatives and continuous engagement. With these emails, you can craft personalised marketing campaigns, unveil special promotions and extend tailored offers. Through these direct connections, you have the power to nurture guest loyalty, inspire repeat bookings and fortify brand affinity.

But that's not all. Booking through your website affords hotels the liberty to provide additional value and benefits. Picture exclusive perks like complimentary room upgrades, early check-ins, late check-outs or an array of additional amenities. These offerings may not be readily available when booking through OTAs. This added value becomes the brushstroke that enhances the canvas of the guest experience, enticing them to return to your hotel's website for future bookings.

In this chapter, you'll uncover the keys to mastering your hotel's website, transforming it into a revenue-boosting powerhouse that sets you on the path to success in the dynamic world of hospitality.

Practical Strategies

Hotels can drive incremental revenue through their website by implementing the following strategies and offers:

1. Convincing more users to book:
- Limited-Time Offers: Create time-sensitive promotions or discounts to create a sense of urgency and encourage immediate bookings.
- Best Rate Guarantee: Assure guests that booking directly on the hotel website offers the best rates compared to third-party platforms.
- Direct Booking Benefits: Highlight exclusive benefits like free Wi-Fi, complimentary breakfast or loyalty program perks for guests who book directly.
- Transparent Booking Process: Clearly display room availability, rates and cancellation policies to instil confidence in potential guests.

2. Convincing users to stay longer:
- Extended Stay Discounts: Offer discounted rates for guests who book longer stays, providing an incentive to extend their visit.

- Additional Night Free: Provide an additional night free of charge for guests who book a certain minimum length of stay.
- Package Inclusions: Create packages that include additional amenities or activities for guests staying longer, such as spa treatments, dining credits, or local experiences.

3. Convincing users to upgrade rooms:
- Upgrade Promotions: Provide special offers or discounts on room upgrades to attract guests to enjoy a more luxurious or spacious accommodation.
- Showcase Room Features: Highlight the unique features and benefits of higher-tier rooms on the website, enticing guests to upgrade for a better experience.

4. Convincing users to book a package:
- Value-Added Packages: Create packages that bundle accommodations with additional perks like spa treatments, airport transfers or dining credits at a discounted price.
- Themed Packages: Design packages centred around special events, holidays or local attractions, offering guests a comprehensive and convenient experience.
- Family or Group Packages: Offer packages specifically tailored for families or groups, including discounted rates, connected rooms or complimentary amenities for children.

It is important for hotels to prominently display these offers on their website, provide clear and detailed information about the benefits and ensure a smooth booking process.

Additionally, implementing effective call-to-action buttons, personalised messaging and targeted email campaigns can further enhance the effectiveness of these offers in driving incremental revenue through the hotel website.

Chapter 4: Key Takeaways

Here are the 10 key takeaways from the chapter on "Driving Incremental Revenue through the Hotel Website":

1. **Direct Bookings Advantage:** Direct bookings through the hotel website save on commission fees, allowing hotels to allocate those savings towards enhancing guest experiences.

2. **Guest Communication:** Booking directly establishes direct communication with guests, enabling opportunities for remarketing and personalised engagement.

3. **Added Value:** Hotels can offer exclusive perks, such as room upgrades, early check-ins and additional amenities, to guests who book through the website, enhancing their experience.

4. **Limited-Time Offers:** Time-sensitive promotions create urgency and encourage immediate bookings, driving revenue growth.

5. **Best Rate Guarantee:** Assure guests that booking on the hotel website offers the best rates compared to third-party platforms, increasing direct bookings.

6. **Extended Stay Incentives:** Offering discounts for longer stays encourages guests to extend their visit and boosts revenue.

7. **Upgrade Promotions:** Special offers on room upgrades entice guests to enjoy more luxurious accommodations, driving additional revenue.

8. **Package Deals:** Bundling accommodations with perks like spa treatments or dining credits at a discounted rate entices guests and adds value.

9. **Themed and Group Packages:** Creating packages centred around special events, holidays or tailored for families/groups offers unique experiences and drives bookings.

10. **Clear Information and Call-to-Action:** Clearly displaying offers, providing detailed information and implementing effective call-to-action buttons enhance the website's ability to drive incremental revenue.

These takeaways highlight the strategic approaches that hotels can use to optimise revenue streams through their websites, encouraging direct bookings, extended stays, room upgrades and package reservations.

Conclusion

As we conclude this chapter, we commend your dedication and successful journey through the art of driving revenue through your hotel's website. You've unlocked the full potential of this powerful channel, recognising it as a beacon of profitability in your toolkit.

Throughout this chapter, you've harnessed the strategies of offering exclusive perks, showcasing benefits and crafting irresistible packages. These tactics serve as the magnetic force that pulls guests toward direct bookings, prolongs their stays and elevates their room experiences.

In your arsenal, you've found powerful allies: personalised offers that resonate with individual guests, strategic marketing that captivates the audience and transparent booking processes that build trust. These strategies not only maximise conversions but also sow the seeds of guest loyalty, fostering a relationship that extends far beyond a single transaction.

As you move forward, remember that the journey is ongoing, and the opportunities are boundless. With each click, each booking and each satisfied guest, your hotel's website becomes a dynamic engine of revenue success in the ever-evolving world of hospitality.

5

Technology and Automation in the Hotel Industry

In the fast-paced and ever-evolving world of hospitality, technology and automation have transcended from being mere tools to becoming indispensable allies. They hold the key to not only enhancing guest experiences but also streamlining operations and unlocking the full potential of revenue.

Within the pages of this chapter, we embark on an exploration of the pivotal role played by technology and automation in the hotel industry. We'll venture into the realms of macro- and micro-data, unravelling their significance. Moreover, we'll dissect the orchestration of various tools that harmonise to craft a comprehensive RevMarketing strategy.

This chapter is your gateway to understanding how the digital age has transformed the hospitality landscape and how you can leverage technology and automation to thrive in this dynamic and competitive environment.

The Power of Technology and Automation

The hotel industry has undergone a significant paradigm shift with the advent of technology and automation. These advancements have not only optimised internal operations but have also revolutionised guest interactions, leading to enhanced guest satisfaction and increased revenue.

This section delves into the multifaceted advantages of integrating technology and automation within the hotel industry.

Streamlined Operations

One of the most immediate benefits of technology and automation is the streamlining of hotel operations. From reservations and check-ins to housekeeping and maintenance, manual processes have been replaced by efficient digital systems. This not only reduces human error but also accelerates processes, allowing staff to focus on more strategic tasks that require human creativity and intuition.

Automated check-in kiosks, for instance, expedite the check-in process, minimising guest wait times and ensuring a smooth arrival experience. Similarly, automated housekeeping management systems optimise room cleaning schedules, leading to quicker room turnover and improved room availability.

Enhanced Guest Experience

Technology has transformed the way guests experience a hotel stay. From the moment a guest makes a reservation, technology plays a crucial role in personalising their journey. Guest preferences are captured and stored in property management systems (PMS), allowing for tailored room assignments, amenity placements and even specific welcome messages upon arrival.

In-room technology, such as smart TVs and integrated control systems, enables guests to customise their environment, creating a more comfortable and convenient stay. Mobile apps offer guests the ability to communicate with the hotel, request services and access information effortlessly.

Automation also enables predictive analytics, allowing hotels to anticipate guest needs and proactively address them.

Data-Driven Insights

Technology generates a wealth of data that, when harnessed effectively, can provide invaluable insights for strategic decision-making. By analysing macro-data such as occupancy rates, demand patterns and market trends, hotels can adjust pricing strategies, optimise inventory and plan for peak seasons.

Micro-data, which includes individual guest preferences, booking behaviours and post-stay feedback, allows hotels to create targeted marketing campaigns and personalised offers. These insights enable a deeper understanding of guest demographics and behaviours, fostering more meaningful connections and loyalty-building efforts.

Revenue Maximisation

Automation, coupled with data analysis, contributes directly to revenue maximisation. Revenue management systems (RMS) utilise historical and real-time data to dynamically adjust room rates based on demand fluctuations, events and market trends. This optimisation ensures that hotels can charge the right price at the right time, ultimately increasing revenue and profitability.

Furthermore, technology-driven marketing initiatives, such as email campaigns and social media promotions, can be tailored to specific guest segments, boosting engagement and conversion rates.

We, at Userguest have gone a step further. Userguest is more than just a tool — it's a paradigm shift in the way revenue and marketing teams collaborate and thrive together. By seamlessly bridging the gap between revenue and marketing initiatives, Userguest places your hotel's revenue strategies front and centre, directly on your website. The tool's data-driven insights guide users towards booking options that enhance your revenue and automatically optimise occupancy.

Userguest brings together revenue and marketing teams under a shared umbrella, empowering them to work collectively towards a common goal: increasing revenue and enhancing guest experiences.

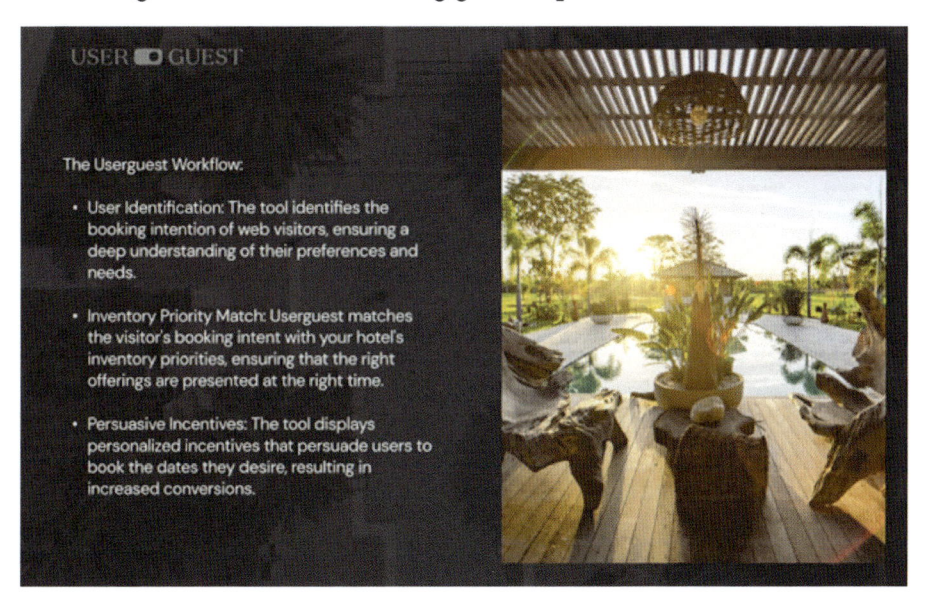

The Userguest Workflow:

- User Identification: The tool identifies the booking intention of web visitors, ensuring a deep understanding of their preferences and needs.
- Inventory Priority Match: Userguest matches the visitor's booking intent with your hotel's inventory priorities, ensuring that the right offerings are presented at the right time.
- Persuasive Incentives: The tool displays personalized incentives that persuade users to book the dates they desire, resulting in increased conversions.

The ability to identify high-value guests and incentivise their loyalty through personalised offers contributes significantly to revenue growth.

Continuous Improvement

Technology and automation facilitate a culture of continuous improvement. Through data analysis and feedback mechanisms, hotels can identify areas for enhancement in real-time. Guest feedback, whether from online reviews or post-stay surveys, can be aggregated and analysed to pinpoint trends and areas of concern.

This data-driven approach enables hotels to refine their services, address pain points and innovate based on evolving guest preferences. The iterative nature of technological integration allows for a dynamic response to changing market dynamics and customer expectations.

The power of technology and automation in the hotel industry is undeniable. From optimising operations and enhancing guest experiences to generating data-driven insights and maximising revenue, these advancements have reshaped the way hotels operate and interact with their guests. As technology continues to evolve, embracing automation and data-driven strategies will remain essential for hotels to stay competitive in a rapidly changing landscape.

Macro-Data and Micro-Data: Unveiling Insights for Revenue and Marketing

In the hotel industry, the successful utilisation of both macro-data and micro-data is pivotal for crafting effective revenue and marketing strategies. These data subsets provide distinct perspectives on industry trends and individual guest preferences, enabling hotels to tailor their offerings and outreach efforts for optimal results.

Macro-Data

Macro-data encompasses large-scale, aggregated information that helps hotels understand industry-wide trends and dynamics. This data is instrumental for making high-level strategic decisions that can impact revenue and marketing efforts. Some key areas where macro-data comes into play include:

> Occupancy and Demand Patterns: Analysing macro-data on occupancy rates, seasonality and historical booking trends provides insights into periods of high demand and low demand. This allows hotels to adjust pricing strategies, offer promotions during off-peak times and maximise revenue during peak seasons.

> Competitor Benchmarking: Comparing macro-data with competitor performance metrics helps hotels assess their competitive position.

This information aids in setting competitive room rates, designing unique value propositions and identifying market gaps.

- Market Trends and Events: Macro-data reveals broader market trends and upcoming events that might influence travel patterns. Hotels can align their marketing efforts with these trends and create targeted packages or experiences to attract specific traveller segments.

- Economic Factors: Monitoring macroeconomic indicators can give hotels a broader understanding of consumers' financial confidence and spending patterns. This information assists in adjusting pricing and marketing strategies based on economic conditions.

Micro-Data

Micro-data focuses on individual guest interactions, behaviours and preferences. This data provides a personalised lens through which hotels can craft tailored experiences and marketing campaigns, fostering guest loyalty and driving revenue. Some ways micro-data enhances revenue and marketing results include:

- Guest Profiles and Preferences: By collecting micro-data on guest preferences, such as room type, amenities and special requests, hotels can ensure a personalised experience. This level of customisation enhances guest satisfaction and encourages repeat visits.

- Booking History and Behaviours: Analysing micro-data related to booking patterns and behaviours helps hotels identify segments of high-value guests. This information guides marketing efforts to target and engage these guests with offers that resonate with their past behaviours.

- Post-Stay Feedback: Micro-data in the form of guest feedback provides valuable insights into service quality and areas for improvement. Hotels can use this data to refine their operations, ensuring that guests' concerns are addressed and positive aspects are amplified.

> Loyalty Program Insights: Micro-data from loyalty program interactions unveils guest engagement levels, preferences and redemption behaviours. Hotels can use this information to create personalised loyalty rewards and incentives that drive repeat business.

Integration for Revenue and Marketing Enhancement

The synergy between macro-data and micro-data is where the true power of data-driven strategies emerges. Here's how the integration of these data subsets can lead to improved revenue and marketing outcomes:

> Dynamic Pricing and Inventory Optimisation: Integrating macro-data from historical occupancy trends with micro-data on guest booking behaviours allows hotels to dynamically adjust pricing and inventory. This ensures optimal room rates that resonate with individual guests and market demands.

> Personalised Marketing Campaigns: By leveraging micro-data insights about guest preferences and behaviours, hotels can create hyper-targeted marketing campaigns. These campaigns can highlight personalised offers, amenities and experiences that resonate with individual guests, driving higher conversion rates.

> Tailored Loyalty Programs: Integrating loyalty program micro-data with macro-data about industry trends enables hotels to refine their loyalty programs. This ensures that the rewards and incentives offered align with both guest preferences and broader market dynamics.

> Feedback-Informed Marketing: Combining micro-data from post-stay feedback with macro-data about industry trends allows hotels to craft marketing narratives that address guest concerns and highlight improvements. This demonstrates a commitment to guest satisfaction and enhances brand reputation.

Conclusion

In the modern hotel industry, technology and automation are revolutionising operations by harnessing both micro- and macro-data.

At the micro level, hotels are utilising guest-specific data, such as individual preferences, booking history and on-site behaviour, to offer personalised experiences. This includes customised room amenities, tailored recommendations and targeted marketing efforts. On the macro scale, data analytics and automation are used to optimise pricing strategies, room allocations and resource management across the entire hotel chain.

By aggregating data from multiple properties, market trends and economic indicators, hotels can make informed decisions to maximise revenue and efficiency. Overall, technology-driven data analysis and automation are reshaping the hotel industry, enabling enhanced guest experiences and improved operational performance at both individual properties and across entire hotel portfolios.

The Interplay of Tools: Orchestrating Data for Optimal Results

In the realm of RevMarketing for hotels, the orchestration of various technology tools forms a dynamic ecosystem that facilitates seamless data flow and drives strategic decision-making.

The interplay between these tools, which encompass property management, customer relationship management, revenue management, marketing automation and data analytics, is crucial for crafting effective and personalised guest experiences while optimising revenue. Let's delve into how these tools interact and synergise for optimal results.

Property Management System (PMS)
The Property Management System (PMS) is the nucleus of hotel operations, serving as the primary repository for guest information,

reservations, check-ins, check-outs and room assignments. Its interaction with other tools is pivotal for efficient data exchange:

- **Customer Relationship Management (CRM) Integration:** The PMS feeds guest booking behaviours and preferences into the CRM. This ensures a comprehensive guest profile that guides personalised marketing efforts and service delivery during the stay.
- **Revenue Management System (RMS) Integration**: By providing real-time occupancy and booking data to the RMS, the PMS enables dynamic pricing adjustments based on room availability and market demand.
- **Marketing Automation Integration**: Integrating the PMS with marketing automation tools ensures that guest data is up-to-date and accurate. This empowers the marketing team to send timely and relevant messages to guests throughout their journey.

Customer Relationship Management (CRM) System

The Customer Relationship Management (CRM) system acts as the brain behind personalised guest interactions, consolidating and analysing guest data to tailor experiences:

- **PMS Integration:** The CRM system synchronises with the PMS to create holistic guest profiles, encompassing booking history, preferences and feedback. This comprehensive view informs marketing efforts and guest engagement strategies.
- **Marketing Automation Integration**: The CRM shares guest segmentation data with marketing automation tools, allowing for targeted campaigns that resonate with individual preferences and behaviours.
- **Data Analytics Integration**: Integrating the CRM with data analytics platforms provides insights into guest behaviour trends and satisfaction levels. These insights drive continuous improvement efforts across all touchpoints.

Revenue Management System (RMS)

The Revenue Management System (RMS) utilises macro-data to optimise pricing strategies and maximise revenue:

- **PMS Integration**: The RMS interfaces with the PMS to gather real-time occupancy data and room rates. This information guides the system in making dynamic pricing decisions based on demand fluctuations.
- **Data Analytics Integration**: Integrating with data analytics tools enriches the RMS with broader market trends and competitor benchmarking insights, enhancing the accuracy of pricing recommendations.

Marketing Automation

Marketing automation tools leverage micro-data to execute personalised campaigns and nurture guest relationships:

- **PMS Integration**: Integrating with the PMS ensures that marketing automation tools access up-to-date guest profiles, allowing for timely and relevant communication.
- **CRM Integration**: The CRM enriches marketing automation efforts by providing insights into guest preferences, enabling personalised offers and messaging that resonate with individual interests.
- **Data Analytics Integration**: Combining marketing automation with data analytics allows hotels to track campaign performance, analyse engagement rates and fine-tune strategies for better results.

Data Analytics and Business Intelligence

Data analytics platforms provide actionable insights by analysing both macro- and micro-data:

- **PMS Integration**: By interfacing with the PMS, data analytics tools access guest demographics, preferences and behaviours, enabling the identification of emerging trends and high-value guest segments.

- **CRM Integration**: The CRM contributes guest interaction data to the analytics platform, painting a comprehensive picture of guest journeys and guiding decisions for process optimisation.
- **RMS Integration**: Integrating with the RMS enriches data analytics with industry-wide occupancy and demand patterns, facilitating the identification of revenue optimisation opportunities.

Conclusion

The interplay of various tools within the RevMarketing ecosystem forms a sophisticated dance that orchestrates the flow of data, insights and actions. By seamlessly integrating property management, customer relationship management, revenue management, marketing automation and data analytics tools, hotels can enhance guest experiences, optimise revenue and drive marketing success. This harmonious integration empowers hotels to create a cohesive strategy that balances high-level industry insights with personalised guest engagement, ultimately leading to sustained growth and customer loyalty.

RevMarketing Automation

In the world of hotel management, revenue and marketing teams traditionally operate in isolation from each other, often with little awareness of each team's activities. This disconnect is a pervasive concern across the industry as it directly impacts a hotel's profitability.

Recently, there has been a noteworthy shift in roles where the responsibilities of revenue management and marketing have converged, resulting in the emergence of the "commercial director" role. While this move toward unity makes sense, not all hotels have the capability or inclination to appoint a commercial director. Nevertheless, the challenge of seamlessly integrating revenue and marketing efforts at the execution level persists.

In response to this challenge, Userguest introduces a groundbreaking concept called RevMarketing Automation (RMA). RMA represents a logical evolution in hotel technology designed to bridge the gap between revenue and marketing.

RMA is designed to help close this gap by empowering revenue and marketing collectively through intelligent automation. By combining the efforts of the hotel revenue manager and the marketing team, RMA helps to align goals and strategies between the two. The solution is not about replacing marketing teams or revenue managers but enabling these teams to work better and smarter together.

Both roles are clearly understood, so what's the missing link? While putting revenue strategies together is an important job, once these are in place, a widespread problem occurs. These strategies are not always presented to the end user! In some cases, they are not leveraged enough to bring real value to the user and/or hotel due to limited digital touchpoints.

Why is RevMarketing Automation necessary?

Revenue management systems (RMS) are typically integrated with the booking engine, not the hotel website.

Guests often land on a hotel's website from various traffic sources, but the conversion to bookings occurs only 20% of the time for many hotels.

In most cases, **a staggering 80% of website visitors drop off at this stage and continue their search elsewhere, primarily due to issues related to website performance and user experience.**

Here's the critical point: during this crucial initial digital interaction, users often encounter no persuasion or incentives to book. All the carefully crafted pricing strategies developed by the revenue team go to waste because users never reach the booking engine.

It's only when users enter their preferred stay dates that they encounter revenue strategies like offers, pricing and incentives. The consequence of potentially losing 80% of website traffic at the vital website stage is substantial as hoteliers miss the opportunity to convert users with enticing offers in 8 out of 10 cases. This missed opportunity in user engagement is detrimental to successful marketing initiatives and overall website performance.

Without access to data from the RMS, optimising marketing campaigns and convincing website visitors to complete bookings become challenging. Marketing investments often prove inefficient due to:

1. Lack of information about room availability during specific periods
2. Redirecting users to unavailable dates
3. Failing to provide incentives or offers to the most profitable markets

How does RMA resolve this crucial gap in the user journey on the hotel website?

So, how can we tackle this problem and make revenue strategies more effective directly on the hotel website? This is where RMA comes into play, implementing intelligent revenue strategies directly on the hotel website. It enables revenue and marketing teams to align by presenting these strategies to users and actively engaging them.

Here's how RevMarketing Automation accomplishes this:

Using a data-centric approach, RMA collects and interprets valuable data from the hotel website, using these insights effectively. When a hotel website, booking engine and hotel PMS are connected through RMA, the user's booking behaviours, demand trends and the hotel's inventory goals align seamlessly.

This means when a hotel website, the booking engine and the hotel PMS are connected via RMA, the user's booking behaviours, demand trends and the hotel's inventory goals are perfectly aligned—just the way they should be.

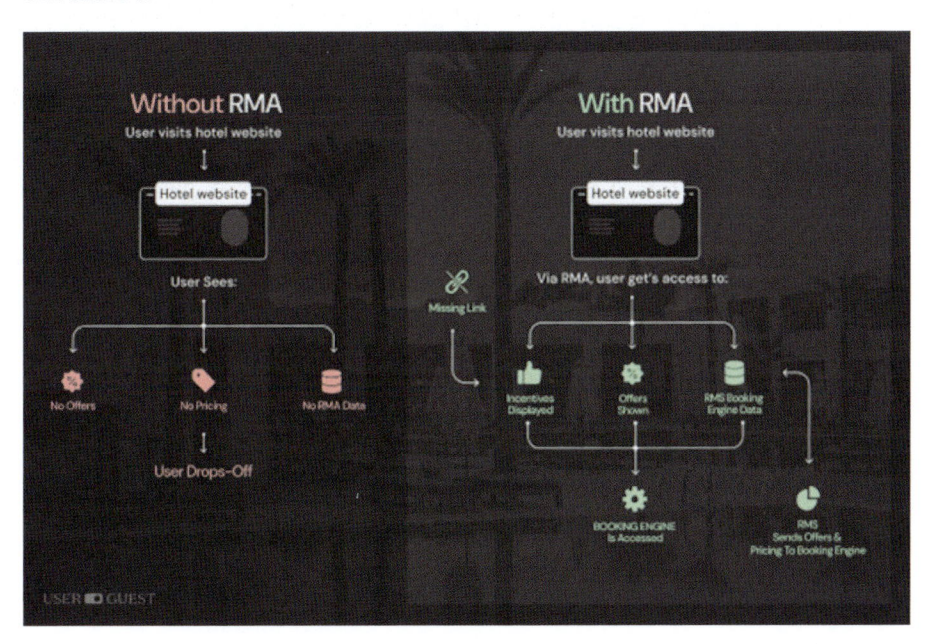

The benefits of RevMarketing Automation

In practice, RMA revolves around identifying revenue opportunities based on a hotel's proprietary data and employing marketing techniques in conjunction with revenue strategies to influence users toward desired outcomes.

RMA strategies can address a multitude of challenges that hotels face daily. Specific strategies can be tailored to meet the hotel's unique needs and objectives. Some examples include:

- Boosting occupancy during low-demand periods
- Upselling during high-demand periods
- Stimulating demand on specific days of the week
- Encouraging longer lengths of stay

In summary, RevMarketing Automation's purpose is to increase revenue for the hotel, increase occupancy where needed, improve Average Daily Rates, extend booking lengths of stay and sell higher category rooms, in line with the hotel's strategy.

How to implement RevMarketing Automation on a hotel website
RMA is a concept that has been developed by Userguest. By adding Userguest's technology to a hotel website, the tool automatically applies the RMA concept and matches the user's booking intent with the hotel's inventory priorities. Ultimately, this unlocks the hotel website and allowing revenue and occupancy to be driven through automated offers and incentives.

In summary, RevMarketing Automation represents a forward-thinking approach to enhancing the synergy between revenue and marketing teams in the hotel industry.

RMA is designed to empower both revenue and marketing teams through intelligent automation, fostering collaboration and synergy between these vital departments. It is essential to emphasise that RMA doesn't seek to replace marketing teams or revenue managers but aims to enhance their effectiveness by ensuring that revenue strategies reach the end user.

RMA addresses the potential loss of website traffic due to limited digital touchpoints during the initial interaction with users by providing visitors with incentives to book when they first visit a hotel's website. RMA uses intelligent revenue strategies directly on the hotel website, aligning user behaviours, demand trends and inventory goals seamlessly.

Chapter 5: Key Takeaways

Here are the 15 key takeaways from the chapter 'Technology and Automation in the Hotel Industry:

1. Technology and automation are essential tools for hotels to improve guest experiences, streamline operations and maximise revenue.
2. Data-driven insights from technology enable strategic decision-making from adjusting pricing strategies to planning for peak seasons.
3. Automation, combined with data analysis, directly contributes to revenue maximisation through dynamic pricing and targeted marketing.
4. Successful hotel revenue and marketing strategies depend on utilising both macro-data and micro-data.
5. Macro-data encompasses industry-wide trends and informs strategic decisions such as pricing adjustments and marketing strategies.
6. Micro-data focuses on individual guest interactions and preferences, enabling personalisation and loyalty-building.
7. Integration of macro and micro-data allows for dynamic pricing, personalised marketing campaigns and feedback-driven improvements.
8. Integration and synergy between tools like Property Management System (PMS), Customer Relationship Management (CRM), Revenue Management System (RMS), Marketing Automation and Data Analytics are essential for personalised guest experiences and revenue optimisation.
9. PMS serves as the core of hotel operations, integrating with CRM to create comprehensive guest profiles, with RMS for dynamic pricing adjustments and with marketing automation for timely guest communication.
10. CRM consolidates and analyses guest data, syncing with PMS and marketing automation for tailored experiences and campaigns.

11. Data analytics platforms enhance RMS, CRM and marketing automation with insights from macro- and micro-data, guiding decisions and optimising revenue and guest engagement.
12. Traditional hotel management sees revenue and marketing teams working in isolation, impacting profitability.
13. Userguest has introduced RevMarketing Automation (RMA) to bridge the gap between revenue and marketing through intelligent automation.
14. RMA aims to align revenue and marketing efforts, enhancing user engagement on hotel websites and optimising marketing campaigns.
15. RMA collects data from hotel websites, booking engines and PMS to align booking behaviours, demand trends and inventory goals, ultimately increasing revenue and occupancy.

Mastering RevMarketing for Hotel Revenue Excellence

Within the pages of this book, we embark on a transformative journey into the realm of RevMarketing – a paradigm shift in the world of hotel revenue generation and marketing. In the following chapters, we'll delve deep into the intricacies of RevMarketing, unveiling how it seamlessly integrates website user experience (UX), website analytics, booking behaviour, revenue management and technology to drive financial success in the competitive hospitality industry.

RevMarketing, short for Revenue Marketing, stands at the heart of our exploration. It signifies a fundamental shift in how hoteliers approach revenue generation and marketing. At its core, RevMarketing orchestrates a harmonious interplay between marketing and revenue management techniques, aligning marketing efforts with overarching revenue objectives.

Key Components of RevMarketing:
- **Website UX (User Experience)**: Your guest's journey often commences on your hotel's website. We'll learn that a user-friendly, engaging website experience is paramount in RevMarketing. It's

about guiding visitors seamlessly through the booking process with analytics serving as your compass for improvements.

- **Website Analytics**: Data is the lifeblood of RevMarketing. Through website analytics, we'll discover how hoteliers gain invaluable insights into user behaviour, preferences and booking patterns. This information directs personalised promotions and offers that resonate with potential guests.

- **Booking Behaviour**: Understanding guest interactions during the booking process is pivotal. By analysing booking behaviour, hoteliers can optimise pricing strategies, adjust room availability and implement upselling tactics to maximise revenue.

- **Data-Driven Insights**: Data is our foundation. We'll explore how collecting and analysing data points, including guest behaviour, market trends and competitor insights, empower data-driven decision-making in both marketing and revenue management.

- **Revenue Objectives Alignment**: We'll emphasise the importance of aligning marketing efforts with revenue objectives. This alignment ensures that marketing campaigns and strategies not only attract guests but also drive revenue growth while preserving profitability.

- **Pricing Strategies**: RevMarketing incorporates pricing strategies into the marketing process. We'll learn how it leverages dynamic pricing, seasonal promotions and rate optimisation to influence guest booking decisions based on pricing dynamics.

- **Targeted Marketing Campaigns**: Personalisation is key in RevMarketing. We'll explore how segmentation and tailored marketing messages and offers to specific customer segments enhance the effectiveness of marketing efforts.

- **Inventory Management**: Effective RevMarketing involves real-time inventory management, adapting to market conditions by adjusting availability and pricing strategies accordingly.

- **Technology Integration**: Technology serves as a vital enabler of

RevMarketing. Automation tools, revenue management systems and CRM software streamline processes and execute marketing campaigns efficiently, allowing hoteliers to respond swiftly to changing market conditions and guest preferences.

In conclusion, RevMarketing represents a holistic approach to hotel revenue generation and marketing. By seamlessly blending data-driven insights, pricing strategies, targeted marketing campaigns and technology, it empowers hoteliers to not only survive but thrive in the dynamic and competitive landscape of the hospitality industry.

As you complete this journey through the world of RevMarketing, you are equipped with the knowledge and skills to harness its power for better profitability. You now understand the importance of integrating website UX, analytics, booking behaviour analysis, revenue management and technology into a coherent strategy that optimises revenue and enhances the guest experience.

Consider this book your certification in this innovative approach, validating your proficiency. RevMarketing is your strategic cornerstone, enabling you to adapt and excel in an ever-changing landscape. Here's to your continued success in maximising hotel revenue and delivering exceptional guest experiences!

Printed in Great Britain
by Amazon